THE FAST AND THE FURIOUS™
ファースト アンド フュリアス

THE OFFICIAL CAR GUIDE
> > > ALL THE CARS, ALL THE MOVIES

Kris Palmer

UNIVERSAL

This edition first published by Haynes Publishing in 2006

Haynes Publishing, Sparkford, Yeovil, Somerset BA22 7JJ, UK
Tel: 01963 442030 Fax: 01963 440001
Int. tel: +44 1963 442030 Int. fax: +44 1963 440001
E-mail: sales@haynes.co.uk
Website: www.haynes.co.uk

A catalogue record for this publication is available from the British Library.

ISBN 1 84425 356 2

On the cover: The 2006 Mitsubishi Evo IX driven by Sean Boswell (played by Lucas Black) in *The Fast and the Furious: Tokyo Drift*.

On the frontispiece: Reiko (played by Keiko Kitagawa) pilots a fast and beautiful sport compact in the newest *The Fast and the Furious* film, helping introduce the sport of drifting to a larger U.S. audience.

On the title pages: The Drift King (played by Brian Tee) getting out of his highly modified Nissan 350Z.

On the back cover: Sean and Twinkie (played by Bow Wow) facing down the Drift King.

About the author

Kris Palmer is a gearhead and freelance writer whose work appears regularly in the *Minneapolis Star Tribune* automotive section and several enthusiast automotive magazines. Palmer also contributed to MBI Publishing Company's highly-regarded *The Cobra in the Barn*. He resides in Minneapolis, Minnesota.

Acquisitions Editor: Lee Klancher
Associate Editor: Leah Noel
Designers: Mandy Iverson and Kou Lor

Printed in China

CONTENTS

FOREWORD

>> When I heard the action for the third *The Fast and the Furious* movie would focus on drifting, I thought, "and what else?" But during production, I had the chance to ride in the car with some of the best drivers in the world, like Rhys Millen, one of the stunt drivers for the film, and it's just amazing.

Once you've done it, you realize how out of control drifting is. The drivers are right on the edge all the time. When you watch it at a distance, it's so graceful, but in the car it's all about doing what the car doesn't want to do. You have rubber flying in your eyes. It's crazy.

The challenge with drifting is the same as with making these films—to take something difficult and make it look easy.

We had a great crew and we pushed each other. It's like when you play sports and you play against people who are better—your game just automatically goes up. I had everything designed, but as soon as I saw how precise and great these drivers were, and how good the crew and cameramen and everybody were, I was redesigning stuff to take advantage of that.

There's one shot where I have Sung Kang standing there with the Evo drifting by him and we were so confident of Rhys that he was literally drifting about six inches from Sung's shin. When you have the camera right there, you really feel it. The wind from the car is blowing Sung's hair around. The drivers were so good that we were able to use angles that I've never really seen before.

To make the film more real, I also wanted to get some of the actors behind the wheel. This was a great cast—young, very talented, very committed. Everybody went and took drifting lessons. Lucas Black (who plays Sean Boswell) and Brian Tee (the Drift King) had a great time throwing the cars around. They were good sports, too.

I like the sense of family that Sean finds in the film. A lot of the characters he hangs around with are at the margin, like him. They're from all over the world, but the car culture brings them together. In a lot of movies when you meet an Asian character, you see a temple or a gong—the role is defined by race in a limited way. These movies are more open and I think viewers will respond to that.

What drew me to the project was the story, which felt like a post-modern Western set in Tokyo—the outsider coming into a strange town to confront others and also to confront himself. He isn't purely good, and the Drift King isn't purely bad. Nothing's that easy or clear cut. You have to make your own choices and live with the decisions you make. I tried to put the viewers in the car with the characters, so they could experience the consequences.

—Justin Lin, director of *The Fast and the Furious: Tokyo Drift*

INTRODUCTION

What Car Movies Are About

>> *The Fast and the Furious: Tokyo Drift* project began for me at Universal just after finishing the film *Jarhead*. Jim Brubaker, president of physical production at Universal Pictures, asked what I knew about the sport of drifting and I put together a book that included the sport's history, evolution, profiles of current drivers, and what cars they chose to drive. This led to me being hired as picture car coordinator for one of the biggest picture car projects to date, *The Fast and the Furious: Tokyo Drift*.

The next step was a trip to Japan to research the sport of drifting. With my co-worker Matt Rubarts, I attended a drifting event and spoke to the competitors and fans (with the help of a translator) to gather as much information as possible. We then began our tour of the best performance shops of Japan, including Top Secret, Veilside, Garageasaurus, and many others.

Upon returning from that first trip, I began working with director Justin Lin and producer Neil Moritz to decide on what vehicles to use. After those decisions were made, it was back to Japan to go shopping. This trip also included a meeting with the group that runs the D1 drifting series and Tsuchiya, aka the Drift King, who agreed to help us with our project. After we purchased over 100 vehicles, it was time to return and set up shop.

We located a large warehouse facility near downtown Los Angeles. We equipped it with everything, from a complete machine shop to our own paint booth. A talented staff of mechanics, fabricators, and body men were put together, and the building process was in motion.

This film was going to put enormous stress on all the cars involved. With drivers like Rhys Millen, Tanner Foust, and other top drift racers, these cars needed to perform like true competition cars. We spent a great deal of time testing cars and finding their weak links to assure the highest level of safety and reliability on set.

The Fast and the Furious: Tokyo Drift was not the first movie I have worked on cars or motorcycles for. In the last five years, the films I have worked on include *Dragonfly, Bruce Almighty, After the Sunset, Meet the Fockers, Jarhead, Batman Begins,* and *Herbie Fully Loaded.*

But *The Fast and the Furious* film series has truly taken the car movie to a new level of excitement and realism. The action in *The Fast and the Furious: Tokyo Drift* will be as close to the real thing as you can get and have on camera. It is this level of realism that sets this film apart.

Drifting is one of the fastest growing segments in the world of motorsports; I think and hope that *The Fast and the Furious: Tokyo Drift* will bring many new fans to this exciting international phenomenon. This is what car movies are all about.

—Dennis McCarthy, *The Fast and the Furious: Toyko Drift* Picture Car Coordinator

PART 1
THE FAST AND THE FURIOUS
(2001)

1995 MITSUBISHI ECLIPSE

DRIVEN BY BRIAN O'CONNER (PLAYED BY PAUL WALKER)

>> Brian O'Conner, played by Paul Walker, is the first main character we meet in *The Fast and the Furious* and he is a cop, not a street racer. But he needs to learn how to drive like the fearless, flat-out speed freaks who race L.A.'s streets in the middle of the night—both in the film and in the real world it explores. He needs to become a credible racer to get close to criminal suspects who are part of that scene.

Brian's ride—to start—is a bright green 1995 Mitsubishi Eclipse, which he launches to a standing quarter-mile in the empty parking lot at Dodger Stadium. Compared to the no-expense-spared street racer engines in some of the film's cars, the Eclipse's 210-horsepower, 2-liter DOHC 4-cylinder is mild. But this is a light car.

Director Rob Cohen wanted to introduce the audience to the white-knuckle, blurred-vision speeds these racers reach on normal roads. By the stadium, Brian winds up the quad-valve, twin-cam mill and guns the Eclipse through the gears past 140 miles per hour. Then O'Conner's out of road. He locks up the low-profile Toyos, sending the Eclipse into a wild triple spin. It squeals to a halt by a guardrail overlooking the skyline of the city whose streets he hopes to conquer. He's not there yet.

As much as their drivers, mechanics, and speed-addicted fans, the cars are stars of the street racing saga. O'Conner's Eclipse, with its fiery lime-green paint and screaming-eagle decal raking down the side, is a sweet ride. Yet against the toughest competition—Dom Toretto, the king of the streets—O'Conner feels it's not enough without more firepower. He tells the speed shop that provides his cover as a parts runner to fix him up with nitrous oxide—two big tanks—before showtime.

The "show" for the Eclipse is O'Conner's street race against Toretto, Edwin, and Danny Yamato. A street-racing novice, O'Conner starts off last as the cars string out in half a flying wedge, with Toretto first, Yamato second, and Edwin third. When he nears the speed he could not control at Dodger Stadium, O'Conner blasts a shot of nitrous. As the compressed nitrous becomes gaseous upon release, it is extremely cold—so cold and oxygen-dense that it allows the engine to burn much more gasoline in each cylinder, and therefore generate much more power. (The same principle of burning more fuel with more oxygen applies to turbocharging and supercharging.) Brian's world bends as Edwin and Yamato move from his future to his past. Another nitrous shot and Brian puts the king of the streets behind him—but only until Toretto hurls his RX-7 into hyperspace with his own shot of nitrous, slipping past the Eclipse to take its pink slip. Though the engine is overheated and the pistons are scorched, the car runs well enough for Brian to escape the swarm of police party-crashers who zero in on the speedfest, picking up Dom along the way.

Sadly, overheating isn't the end of the car's problems. O'Conner and Toretto stray into gangster Johnny Tran's territory—and receive a hostile reception. Tran and his cousin leave momentarily but return to make their point more clearly: Toretto is not allowed in their domain. They unleash a barrage of machine-gun fire that rips holes in the Eclipse's beautiful metal and paintwork. The bullets spark a blaze that hunts down the car's fuel tank and blows a showpiece Eclipse into the tuner afterlife. Such is life when you cross the wrong crowd on an L.A. night—at least in the movies.

Building his next ride, a twin-turbo 1994 Supra, Brian moved closer to Toretto and the inside of the street-racer world.

Although details like the graphics and window tint were changed, most of the cars in *The Fast and the Furious* were based on real cars, including the Eclipse. In fact, this car was rented from L.A. tuner John Lapid. The car shown close up on screen was not actually turbocharged, even though the movie's dialog said it was.

The back of the Eclipse at rest. Big wings and performance exhaust systems are tuner trademarks. Some enthusiasts like to advertise their car's performance with numerous flashy touches, while others don't let on how much they've got under the hood.

Tinted windows allowed for some variation in the interiors of the various duplicate cars used during filming and also hid incorrect faces when stunt drivers had the wheel.

ENGINE:
4G63T quad-valve, DOHC, 2-liter 4-cylinder, with 210 horsepower

BODY MODS:
Robo Car Aero Armor Eclipse kit (including front bumper, side skirts, rear bumper); custom-made carbon-fiber front splitter; custom GT-style roof scoop; ARP two-level GT2-style wing; carbon-fiber race mirrors; shaved door handles; 1997-spec Eclipse headlights; green neon lighting

SPECIALTY MODS:
Sparco racing seats; GReddy temperature and turbo gauges; dual NOS tanks; built-in video monitor; alloy shift knob; drilled alloy racing pedals

WHEELS:
SE7EN 18-inch wheels by Axis Sport Tuning, Inc.

TIRES:
Toyo 225/40/ZR18

SUSPENSION MODS:
Stock

PAINT COLOR:
House of Kolor Bright green

DOUBLES CONSTRUCTED:
5

The filmmakers' attention to detail extends to the top of the vehicle, ensuring a "star" look. Only the taped-up roof scoop gives away that feature's cosmetic nature.

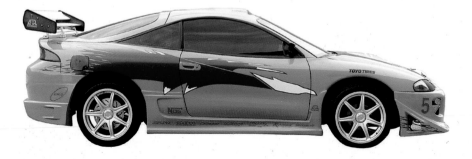

Body kits play a key role in distinguishing the film's cars from their factory counterparts. O'Conner's Eclipse has a custom look from all angles—front, side, rear end, and top.

TOP: Custom wheels also go a long way in setting one car's profile apart from another's. The Eclipse's 18-inch rims, along with Toyo tires, offered strong grip and good airflow to cool the brakes.

MIDDLE: The roof scoop was nonfunctional and taped over during much of filming. Gaffer's tape comes in handy in many ways on the set and is all but undetectable except to those who already know it's there.

BOTTOM: It's a sad, but essential byproduct of most car movies: Some vehicles get destroyed, by design or through punishing stunts. In *The Fast and the Furious,* the script included a crime-story angle, featuring gangster Johnny Tran. When he and his cousin shoot up the Eclipse, it explodes.

1993 MAZDA RX-7 TWIN TURBO

DRIVEN BY DOMINIC TORETTO (PLAYED BY VIN DIESEL)

>> This nitrous-boosted, twin-turbocharged, third-generation RX-7 was the fastest car in L.A.—the machine that made Dominic Toretto the king of the streets. Our first good look at it comes in a four-car street race late at night. Brian O'Conner bets his pink slip—the title to his lime-green Eclipse—that he can beat Dominic, played by Vin Diesel, and the rest of the competition in this car. Bold move.

As the four cars pull into a wide stretch of L.A. pavement, two sexy women dash across the street from opposite sides spraying down an impromptu starting line. Dominic slides back a false vinyl cover and flips up the passenger seat to reveal the RX-7's four-tank NOS system and gauges. As they gun the engines for the start of the race, all four cars spit flames from their tailpipes—a brief glimpse of the explosive fury about to be unleashed under these illegal street racers' hoods. (Take note that the flames are not the nitrous oxide burning. Nitrous is not flammable, though at high temperatures the oxygen in it will separate out and accelerate combustion.)

There is no flag to start the race. Instead, according to custom, a race fan, in this case Hector, holds his hands high overhead, then throws them down for all-throttles deep-sixed.

In the next part of the scene, director Rob Cohen enhanced the link between man and machine with a shot that follows Dominic's arm dropping the RX-7 into first gear, then passes inside the transmission, tracing the shafts to the rotary engine where the wide-open fuel dump bursts to life, force-fed by the twin-turbos' whirring turbines. This horsepower depth-charge breaks the 9.5-inch Toyos free and kicks the car sideways at the start of a no-holds-barred road-rocket showdown.

Cohen enhanced the race footage with digital effects to approximate the sensation of being bent out of shape by a car built for no purpose other than throwing its driver at maximum warp down a city street in the dead of night—winner take all. Apart from the special effects, whose accuracy only a street racer would appreciate, the scene was very true to life, incorporating actual street racers and fans as the bulk of the crowd. The director's vision was shaped by a real race he watched on L.A. streets at 2 a.m. The passion, power, and collective love of the street-race culture he witnessed that night convinced him that the fast and furious street racing lifestyle had to be brought to the big screen.

When the police come at the end of this scene and the crowd vaporizes into the surrounding city, many of the actors behind the wheel are real street racers in their own cars, breaking it loose to recreate this frequent flight from the road rules' enforcers. The stunt coordinator was concerned about unleashing some 200 cars with drivers other than professional stuntmen, but Cohen's faith was rewarded. This crowd of genuine lead-foots fled without a scratch—repeating a scatter-dance they had practiced many times before, without a movie camera to capture it.

The RX-7 is the star of the first race scene, outpacing its rivals thanks to Dominic's deft driving and the car's top-shelf build sheet. It was a hit with the film's car-builders, too. As one of the fastest cars prepped for the film, the RX-7 was a favorite ride for builder Eddie Paul's auto body and fabrication crew. After taking it out for a few spins, they left pronounced burnout marks leading out of his El Segundo, California, shop and up the street.

Toretto's RX-7 was fashioned after a real car owned by Keith Imoto, who at the time worked for a popular tuner in North America. The car came to the film with a full roll cage, but Vin Diesel's large stature combined with the Mazda's cramped cockpit meant something had to go.

The Veilside body kit, custom headlights, and dagger-spoke wheels made Toretto's machine easily recognizable. A cool detail captured in this photo is the nose piece's treatment of the turn-signal lamp, which seems to float in its opening.

The rear wing complements the third generation RX-7's flowing lines—blending aerodynamics with a predatory hint of shark.

1993 MAZDA RX-7 TWIN TURBO SPECIFICATIONS

ENGINE:
Stock twin-turbocharged Mazda rotary with 255 horsepower

BODY MODS:
Veilside USA Aero Body kits; Lexan headlight covers; RX-7 GT rear wing; aluminum struts

SPECIALTY MODS:
Car in four-car race has four-bottle NOS system

WHEELS:
Veilside USA 18x8.5-inch front, 18x9.5-inch rear

TIRES:
Toyo 235/40/ZR18, 255/35/ZR18

SUSPENSION MODS:
Stock

PAINT COLOR:
House of Kolor Fire engine red

DOUBLES CONSTRUCTED:
4

Black accents tie the special headlights into the custom RX-7. The stock car has flip-up lights, a look the studio went back to for the second film. In the sequel, some of the RX-7s that appeared in *The Fast and the Furious* were reused—in duly modified form.

Director Rob Cohen wanted the cars to stand out from their surroundings, as Toretto's car does here in front of corrugated steel siding. Production staff actually repainted homes in plainer colors in some shooting locations so the cars would be more prominent. If homeowners liked the original colors, the studio repainted them after shooting.

Special graphics set the four-wheeled stars of *The Fast and the Furious* apart from every other modified car out there.

The RX-7's special headlights used Lexan covers shaped to body contour. The driver's side cover is cloudy in this photo—a detail that would never be evident on screen. Much more prominent here is the car's hungry look, which was matched by outstanding performance.

1996 ACURA INTEGRA

DRIVEN BY EDWIN (PLAYED BY JA RULE)

>> Driving music—not just music to drive by, but music that drives the film—is a critical element in *The Fast and the Furious* movies and an important part of the import tuner scene. These modern-day hot rods are products of the high-tech age, where builders incorporate sound systems as potent as the engines that blast them to 150 miles per hour and beyond.

Director Rob Cohen wanted rave music, or "pulsing electronica," to create the street-racing environment's high-energy feel. *The Fast and the Furious*' producer, Neal Moritz, thought hip-hop star Ja Rule could connect the film to the real music scene, both as a musical contributor and a character in the story. Ja Rule joined the cast as Edwin, who squares off in a four-way race near the start of *The Fast and the Furious*.

Edwin takes on Toretto, undercover cop Brian O'Conner (racing as Brian Spilner), and street racer Danny Yamato. They've all put money in as the prize for winning, except for O'Conner, who bets his pink slip. Edwin gets a special incentive to win from his girlfriend, Monica, who promises that if he wins, he can have not only her but another vivacious feline who blows him a kiss from the crowd. But this night does not belong to Edwin. O'Conner takes him and Yamato with two shots of nitrous, while Toretto wins with a better-timed nitrous shot closer to the finish.

Movie-car builder Eddie Paul and his crew made four doubles of Edwin's car for the film. (Filmmakers need enough versions of a "star" car to cover stunts, photo shoots, close-up footage of actors in the cars, promotional appearances, and downtime from damage during shooting and transportation.) Paul and a crew of builders were able to use cars from 1994 to 1996 because Acura made few changes to the Integra during this period. They added body kits, a rear wing, special wheels, paint and graphics, plus a wide-open sound system befitting a hip-hop star. As sometimes happens, no footage featuring the car's explosive stereo made the final cut. Because the car had tinted windows, these were held in with gaffer's tape during shooting so they could be quickly removed to allow for shots of Edwin at the wheel.

Despite its relatively brief appearance, Edwin's Integra is one of the most heavily modified cars in the film.

The Acura's body-color Wings West piece is another take on the tuner trademark rear wing. This design has an appealing balance between forward-leaning support struts and rearward-angled sides.

ENGINE:

1.8-liter DOHC, quad-valve B18C1 four-cylinder; AEM cold air intake system; AEM 3-mm overbored throttle body; AEM Tru Time adjustable cam timing gears; AEM Type-R intake cam; AEM overdrive pulleys—alternator and power steering—red anodized; AEM fuel rail, fuel pressure regulator, and fuel filter; DC Sports headers and exhaust system; GReddy engine oil cooler; MSD 6A ignition unit and external HVC blaster coil; Exedy racing clutch and lightweight flywheel; Nology hot wires and Silverstone S3F spark plugs

BODY MODS:

Wings West RS Racing Series ground effects kit, NATCC touring car wing with brake light and front grille, EPH Motorsports carbon-fiber front air dam splitters, Modern Image graphic design and decals

SPECIALTY MODS:

Neuspeed Schroth auto control seat belts, transmission short shifter, and embroidered floor mats; MOMO seat belt shoulder pads and racing pedals; Acropolis USA racing seats (yellow and red) with side mounts and seat sliders; Wedge Engineering MOMO racing seat base mounts; DC Sport billet oil cap, billet plug wire cover, and billet battery tie-down; Grant racing transmission shift knob; GReddy/Trust oil pressure gauge, oil temperature gauge, and water temperature gauge; Performance Techniques billet radiator cap and billet clutch reservoir cap; Purosil yellow vacuum and engine hoses; Folia Tec brake caliper paint; DTM exhaust pipe design film, race tow ring, driver and passenger side floor kick panels, red leather steering wheel cover, and carbon fiber design film; PIAA Super White headlights and high-beam lights; NR white gauge faces; Do-Luck rear cross bar with mounting brackets; Grillcraft custom front grille; EPH Motorsports billet engine bolts and washers; Ignited engine start switch; Auto Image clear red rear tail lamps; Magic aluminum hood speed lifts; Street Glow under-car lights; California Car Cover chrome fire extinguisher; engine compartment fuel pressure gauge

AUDIO:

Sony CDX-C7050X stereo and CD player with removable face; MTX Blue Thunder Pro 752 Power Amp (280 watts); Polk MOMO front speaker set, dX6 rear speakers, and MM100-10 sub woofer; AIResearch Q-Form front kick panels; Street Wires battery cables and terminals

WHEELS:

MOMO GT 17x7.5-inch, 40-mm offset with red socket lugs

TIRES:

Michelin Pilot Sport Tires 215/40/ZR17

SUSPENSION MODS:

Energy Suspension hyperflex polyurethane bushing set with engine-mount bushings; Specialty Products camber adjustment kits; Neuspeed Race lowering springs (2.5 inches), rear upper tie bar, front upper tie bar, rear lower tie bar, rear 19-mm sway bar, stainless-steel brake lines, rear large rotors, and hats for stock brake calipers; Koni adjustable shocks; Axxis Metal Master rear brake pads; Porsche Boxster front brake pads; ATE Blue brake fluid; four-piston Brembo calipers with 11.75-inch slotted rotors (for front brakes)

PAINT COLOR:

House of Kolor Red

DOUBLES CONSTRUCTED:

4

This is one of the surviving Eclipses used for the beauty shots. The color and graphics were simple and bright, making it easy to clone and quick to produce. It took about two days to make each of them. The black tape around the windows allowed them to be removed and replaced quickly so the director could shoot inside the car.

1994 TOYOTA SUPRA

DRIVEN BY BRIAN O'CONNER (PLAYED BY PAUL WALKER)

>> The Supra enters *The Fast and the Furious* after Brian O'Conner, who has infiltrated the illegal street-racer scene as Brian Spilner, goes for broke in a four-car race that includes the king of the streets, Dom Toretto. O'Conner throws down the pink slip for his Eclipse, but Toretto's nitrous-injected, twin-turbo RX-7 is too much. No keys change hands, however—not yet.

The police get wind of the race and the drivers have to scramble. Toretto slips into a parking ramp just ahead of watchful law-enforcement eyes, but he comes out walking and officers recognize him. O'Conner picks him up, shakes the men in blue with some pursuit-style driving, and things look calm. Too bad he's taken them into a part of the city controlled by gangster Johnny Tran—a place where by mutual agreement Toretto is not welcome. Tran and his cousin let the trespassers live, yet they destroy the Eclipse with a shower of machine-gun fire. The king of the streets and young upstart O'Conner arrive at Toretto's house in a taxi.

To honor his lost bet, O'Conner promises Toretto a 10-second car—a street-race machine that can eat up a quarter-mile of pavement in 10 seconds or less. What he brings to Toretto's shop doesn't even look close to the promised debt. Unable to move under its own power, the Supra he tows to Toretto's looks like it fell off a truck, then fell off a cliff. The hood's sprung, the windshield's knocked in, the windshield frame is bent, the passenger door is creased vertically and popped several inches open to the back, and the back bumper is gone and so are the taillights. It's junk-yard fresh. But there's a secret beneath the dust and twisted metal: a 2JZ engine. As Jesse, Toretto's speed whiz buddy, explains on seeing the surprise motor, "this car will decimate all, with about 15 grand in it—or more—worth of speed parts from Japan."

Fortunately for the production, a tricked-out Supra was already available with ample speed goodies from Californian Craig Lieberman. The studio rented Lieberman's car, changed the color, and added some eye-catching graphics. In the film, O'Conner, Toretto, his girlfriend Letty, and Jesse build up and paint O'Conner's new ride to compete in Race Wars, the desert street-racer showdown. As a little frosting on the cake, O'Conner and Toretto square up with a Ferrari at an intersection after the Supra's transformation. When the pompous owner lets O'Conner know his Italian sports car is more than O'Conner can afford, what can Toretto do but tell his friend to "smoke 'im?" Though he takes on some oncoming traffic to do it, O'Conner outpaces his high-brow rival in a true show of how these ramped-up road rockets can move. Sure the Ferrari's a fast car, but some of these street racing machines have double its horsepower and no more weight. That's the beauty of the street-racer scene—a young driver who may never work in a corner office in a silk suit can build a car that leaves a

high-roller in his six-figure sports car choking on fumes with a turbo whine ringing in his ears as the faster ride's taillights fade into the horizon.

O'Conner's Supra doesn't square off in Race Wars because what he's working undercover to stop goes down during the event: Toretto and his criminal associates take off to pull one last job—robbing a tractor trailer right on the highway, looking for a payoff to retire on. O'Conner and Toretto's sister, Mia, blast through the desert zeroing in on a location trace of Toretto's cell phone. O'Conner's given up his undercover identity to Mia to help her stop what even she knows is a very dangerous gambit. The job goes south, though, as Toretto's lifelong friend Vince needs an airlift because he's been shot, and Mia, Dom, Letty, and Leon take off.

The Supra has a final scene in the film: a drag race against Toretto's blown Hemi Charger. Toretto flips and crashes, and police sirens rise in the distance. O'Conner puts his loyalty to a friend over his loyalty to the force and gives Toretto the Supra's keys— honoring his debt for a 10-second car. The hero's 1994 Supra becomes the anti-hero's getaway car. Toretto's time as the king of the streets is over. He takes the car, which he helped build, to pursue his fortunes elsewhere, beyond the racing scene he rose to dominate and the police force looking to put him in a locked cell.

O'Conner's turbo Supra belonged to the film's technical advisor, Craig Lieberman. It came to the production in kandy yellow with a "very sedate" rear spoiler. The production team changed the paint, wheels, body kit, and added the graphics—a joint effort between graphic designer Troy Lee and art director Waldemar Kalinowski.

The turbo Supra is a potent car with an engine that can be tweaked to near absurd horsepower levels. This is about the only view a lot of challengers get once the cars are in motion.

The Supra's hood and front-end kit are well ventilated because the car's high-performance forced-induction engine pulls in a lot of air.

ENGINE:

2JZ 3-liter twin cam, 24-valve inline six; Turbonetics T-66 ball bearing turbo and Delta II wategate; RPS stainless-steel/HTC-coated custom header; NOS 100-horsepower nitrous oxide system; AEBS turbo downpipe; GReddy Power Extreme exhaust system; Pro-Fec B boost controller; Airinx intake, steering wheel–mounted boost remote control, cam gears, power pulleys, front-mount intercooler, oil cooler kit, turbo timer, and boost; EGT oil pressure and water temperature gauges; A'PEXi blowoff valve; HKS vein pressure converter, graphic control computer, and injector pulse monitor; G-Force Engineering racing ROM; Hose Technologies silicone hose kit; Clutchmasters stage III racing clutch and 11-pound billet flywheel; Powerhouse Racing ported/polished throttle body and racing cylinder head work (port/polish)

BODY MODS:

Bomex front spoiler and side/rear skirts; TRD composite hood; ARP aluminum bi-plane rear wing

SPECIALTY MODS:

Stitchcraft Viper blue suede upholstery; Sparco Pista racing seats, steering wheel, and harnesses; MFS custom-built roll cage; custom matching fabric with harness holes and carbon-fiber dash trim

AUDIO/VIDEO:

Clarion VRX8271 in-dash TV/CD changer controller, remote-controlled VMA6481 6-inch wide-screen TV monitor in passenger airbag cavity, VMA9181 5.5-inch TV monitor in trunk area, DSP9300 digital sound processor with parametric EQ/surround sound, CDC 635 CD changer, and SRS 691 6.5-inch separates; Image Dynamics 6-inch separates and 12-inch woofers (2); Phaze Audio TD1500 tube driver amplifiers (2) and TD475 tube driver amplifier; Sony Playstation 1 and 2/DVD; Minolta 6450 VHS-C camcorder; custom-built electric-blue neon tubes for sound system backlighting; system design and fabrication by Audio Options

WHEELS:

M5Tuners 19-inch Dazz/Racing Hart, 19x8.5-inch front, 19x9.5-inch rear

TIRES:

Yokohama AVS S1 275/30/ZR19 and 245/35/ZR19

SUSPENSION MODS:

Eibach coil-over suspension, sway bars, and energy suspension urethane bushings

PAINT COLOR:

House of Kolor Lamborghini Diablo Candy Pearl Orange

DOUBLES CONSTRUCTED:

4

Though barely noticeable here, the Supra has a nice feature for shooting stars like Paul Walker and Vin Diesel inside the car: a targa top.

The ARP rear wing has an aircraft aspect to it that complements the Supra's high-tech look.

The graphics were wilder than what was common in the tuner scene at the time—but not too wild, as the cars' looks were widely copied by enthusiasts all over the world.

1970* DODGE CHARGER

DRIVEN BY DOMINIC TORETTO (PLAYED BY VIN DIESEL)

>> Dominic's father's blown Hemi Charger is an imposing beast of a machine with a pivotal role in the first film. Not only does it play the role of black horse—the anti-hero's steed in his showdown with the hero in the final drag race— it is also a fundamental piece of who Dom Toretto is or, more accurately, what he has become.

Toretto's police file contains the photos of a brutally beaten man Toretto nearly killed with a wrench after the man put Dom's father into the wall on a racetrack and ended his life. The man suffered brain damage, lost an eye, and could work only as a maintenance man after the attack. It is the one moment in his life Toretto would take back if he could—but no one gets that chance.

O'Conner has earned enough of Toretto's trust to hear this story. The thrill of speed and the strong bonds of friendship and loyalty he has seen in the street-racer community have changed O'Conner's perspective on the people whose company he entered as an undercover cop looking to bring someone down. O'Conner respects Toretto for the father-figure role he plays to a band of misfit racers and car builders who would probably be on the street or in jail without him. Hearing Dom's remorse for his brutal assault makes O'Conner understand Toretto all the more—enough to help him when his time runs out and Toretto's secret life as a modern-day stagecoach robber comes to light.

Toretto has never driven the 900-horsepower Charger until the truck robbery goes bad and he and his friends need to blow town. O'Conner comes to bust him, but gangster Johnny Tran arrives pursuing Jesse, who has lost his pink slip and run scared with his car back to Toretto. Tran and his cousin attack with automatic weapons, spraying Toretto's yard and driveway with bullets and killing Jesse. O'Conner takes off after the shooters in his rocket-fast Supra and Toretto joins the chase in the awesome Charger. The gunmen are on motorcycles. Toretto slaps one down with the side of the Hemi Mopar and O'Conner shoots Tran off his bike.

The Supra and Charger then meet on a strip of road Toretto used to drag on in high school—one with a perfect quarter-mile stretch of pavement and a traffic light, currently red, at the finish. When the streetlight flashes to green, Toretto cuts the Hemi-mill loose. The nose rises in a wheelie, and old and new muscle meet in a dead heat. They narrowly miss a train (perhaps a little nod to the train-wreck demise of Peter Fonda's Charger in *Dirty Mary and Crazy Larry*), but a semi trailer crosses the intersection, sending Toretto and his father's drag car flipping over O'Conner's Supra. The Charger slams into the pavement front end first and rolls, buckling the hood and turning the front wheels under. The car's done and Toretto's hurt, but O'Conner doesn't send his troubled friend to jail. Instead, he honors his bet. He throws his keys to Dom, who disappears just like his sister Mia, the woman who has won O'Conner's heart.

Universal Studios built several Chargers for the film. The one we see in the barn contains a blown 426 Hemi powerplant and combines parts from 1969 and 1970 models. Such mergers are not uncommon in the Mopar world, where Charger values—especially Hemis—have soared to the cost of modern supercars. The 1969 and 1970 share the bar taillight across the back, while only the 1970 wears the chrome ring around the nose, doubling as the car's bumper.

The car destroyed in the jump is not, of course, a real Hemi, but a big-block car with a cosmetic blower attached to the hood. There was also a trick car with twin bars hinged at the back and attached to a nitrogen-gas lift. The bars had

small wheels on them, which struck the ground and lifted the Charger's front end off the ground in a controlled wheelie when activated by the stunt driver. Real tire smoke—along with a bit more added as a special effect in post-production—hid the trick mechanicals for the final cut.

If original *Dukes of Hazzard* fans thought this jumping black Charger soared much like the ol' General Lee, there's a connection there: Eddie Paul, whose team revamped the bodies of cars for *The Fast and The Furious* and *2 Fast 2 Furious*, designed and built pipe ramps for the popular TV show and also worked on it as a stuntman early in his career.

A classic showdown of old muscle and modern high-tech performance. The Charger is cheating on the wheelie, which was produced through bars hinged at the back of the car and connected to a driver-operated gas lift. The passenger-side bar is visible just ahead of the tire smoke.

1970* DODGE CHARGER SPECIFICATIONS
*(BUILT FROM 1969 AND 1970 PARTS)

ENGINE:
426 Hemi for close-up shots; other cars used big-block 440 motors

BODY MODS:
Stock body with cutout hood on real supercharged car and fake superchargers bolted to other cars' hoods

WHEELS:
American Racing Torq Thrust five-spoke

TIRES:
Mickey Thompson ET Street Drag

SPECIALTY MODS:
Special lift mechanism fitted to wheelie car as described in text

PAINT COLOR:
House of Kolor Black

DOUBLES CONSTRUCTED:
4

Ouch! The jumped car was junk after it slammed into the pavement. You can see the whole front end twisting and buckling on impact. This was a rough car dressed up for the stunt, but a Mopar fan still feels the Charger's pain.

EDDIE PAUL

Car customizer for The Fast and the Furious *and* 2 Fast 2 Furious

In addition to customizing the cars for the first two *The Fast and The Furious* films, Eddie Paul has contributed numerous machines and devices to many well-known movies and TV series. Along with his work as fabricator, inventor, builder, and customizer, he has served as stuntman, second unit director, trainer, or advisor on many projects. *Eddie Paul*

>> For most of us, a feature film experience transpires for 90 to 120 minutes as we sit in a comfortable chair. Yet the actions that unfold on screen are the result of a process that can take years and involves the efforts of dozens—even hundreds—of people. Actions, characters, and the devices they use appear and behave as they do not by luck or by chance, but because creative people worked tirelessly to achieve those results.

For 37 years, Eddie Paul has been one of those creative forces, building and often operating devices that make memorable scenes possible. During three-and-half decades in the film and TV business, he has built machines to drive, fly, jump, swim, and crash, to emulate an existing car or truck, or animal, or to look like nothing else of its kind. In a business with unusual needs and high expectations, Paul is a go-to guy—the bigger the challenge, the better. Picking up the gauntlet as stuntman, stunt coordinator, second-unit director, inventor, fabricator, designer, and builder has tried Paul's stamina with sleepless nights and intense physical challenges (some leading to broken bones).

What sets this restless, inventive mind apart from most others is that Paul dropped out of high school. While this is a setback for some, for Eddie Paul it was sign of his desire to get things done. What is school, after all, but learning what other people have already learned before you? Paul cut out the middleman in search of a fresh challenge. Some people confronted by a task grow uneasy if it hasn't been done before, but Eddie Paul delights in unique tests of his creativity and skills.

Hollywood found this able creator by accident in 1970. A film crew was shooting by Paul's autobody shop when a car involved in the shoot was damaged. The man overseeing the car, David Marder, came to Paul's shop and asked if he could fix it by the following day. It was the beginning of a long and fruitful relationship. Working through the night, Paul and an employee had the car ready to go by morning—and Marder had a new name for his Rolodex.

If one car in one night is a challenge, how about four dozen in two weeks? That was Paul's task on the film, *Grease*, for which he restored and customized 48 vintage cars, including the main stunt cars for the race sequence. He shaved off a little extra sleep during that fortnight to fabricate flame-thrower exhaust pipes for the custom black Mercury.

Cars came to the film set in many states, from junker muscle cars built up for destructive stunts, to stock machines fresh from a dealer or private owner and performance tuners rented for the duration of the film. Paul and his crew helped give each car its unique look and made its duplicates identical for filming. *Eddie Paul*

When Marder signed onto *The Fast and the Furious*, he knew what number he would dial for help modifying over 80 cars. Paul's mind was breaking down the job into manageable pieces before he hung up the phone. With assistance from a half-dozen employees, Paul bought most of the film's 84 cars. Over the next two months, he and his crew—coordinating with studio mechanics, advisors, artists, and producers—transformed the vehicles from anonymous daily drivers into unique, eye-catching, street-racing machines.

For *2 Fast 2 Furious*, Marder served as production supervisor and Paul again joined the fray. He and his crew worked on many of the film's cars. Paul's unique fabrication talents shone through in such touches as the transparent, louvered Lexan hood on Slap Jack's turbo Supra and a unique "gator-back" scoop setup on Tej's Acura NSX. Although the NSX appears only briefly when O'Conner and Pearce pull up to Tej's riverfront shop, the work is still a point of pride for Paul.

The Fast and the Furious cars were a sizeable undertaking, but they were no more difficult than many of the things Paul takes on. When *Mask of Zorro* producers wanted some mechanical horses to jump from a bridge into a river, Paul built them. The Cousteau family asked him for a mechanized shark that could swim with real ones and be used for filming, and Paul produced a lifelike, air-powered, 10-foot great white. The diver-operator inside could navigate the beast by looking at an interior monitor that showed a view taken by a camera hidden inside a fake remora fish attached to the shark.

Paul's touch appears on many things that have become part of popular TV and movie culture. He painted one of the original General Lees and many cars throughout the weekly *Dukes of Hazzard* shows (and became a stuntman on the series); he also built the Jeep Mindy drives in the opening sequence of the quirky TV classic *Mork & Mindy*. He created the Quantum Strata Cycle, used by the Power Rangers in that acrobatic, sci-fi kids show, and the special Ford van used in the rescue scene in *E.T.*

Paul has built machines and performed stunts in water, on land, and in the air—but not without cost. While the hobby was in its infancy around 1970, Paul built a hang glider from aluminum and plastic. He jumped off a 100-foot cliff and rose with the high wind, until a sharp gust snapped the wings. He broke countless bones on impact, including his neck. He was in a coma for two weeks, the hospital for six months, and a wheelchair for six more months. He broke his neck again in the late 1990s as a stuntman for a Hyundai Tiburon commercial. The ad showed the car rising out of water behind two fishermen talking in a boat. But the car hit a cable underwater and when Paul was thrown out, his weight belt got caught and came off. He rose to the surface quickly and a camera boat, hurrying to the scene, struck him in the head. Luckily—as with the first break—the injury did not leave Paul paralyzed. It did, however, cause his wife Renee to say "no more stunts."

Paul quickly replaced that work with other projects. He has over a dozen patents under his belt (even his daughter Ariel has one, for an anti-skid device on automobiles, which she applied for at age 9). He's a diver, driver, pilot, motorcycle builder, and instructor for many films and videos.

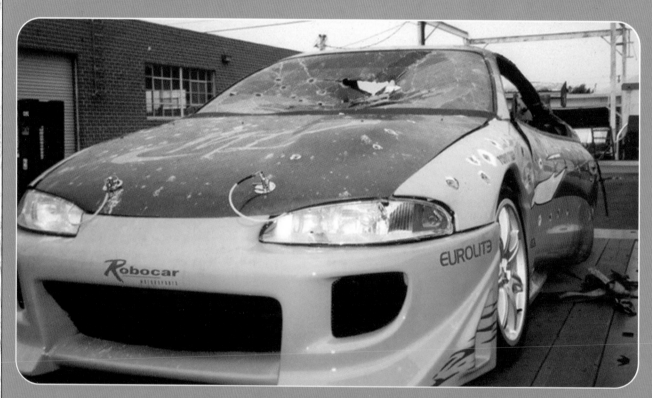

You can't get too attached to work you do for a film production. Some cars, like this Eclipse, get banged up or destroyed, either on purpose, as here, or during the course of punishing stunts. *Eddie Paul*

His current projects include building full-size versions of animated autos that star in the Pixar movie, *Cars*. The studio will take these creations to shows to promote the film. Building the cars involves cutting the plugs from wood with a 3-D router, then using them as contour for a vacuum-formed plastic skin. The body then goes on a real chassis, one of which is a new Porsche 911's—yes, even an Eddie Paul cartoon car means business.

A mechanical great white shark Paul built for a Cousteau family film project served its job well, swimming with real sharks and eventually becoming the subject of a planned attack. *Eddie Paul*

DAVID MARDER

Transportation coordinator/production supervisor

>> *The Fast and the Furious* movies showed us the racing scenes of Los Angeles, Miami, and Tokyo—not in documentary style, but one aimed to accentuate worlds where cars are kings. To create those worlds, cameras recorded a carefully orchestrated fiction played out by hundreds of people, vehicles, equipment, and machines that appeared like a foreign invasion, did their work, then departed in the same lumbering cavalcade that brought them there.

One of the people who helped make sure the cars were ready for their scenes in *The Fast and the Furious* and *2 Fast 2 Furious* was David Marder. As the transportation coordinator for *The Fast and The Furious* and production supervisor for *2 Fast 2 Furious*, he made sure the car stars of both films showed up for work promptly and consistently—despite the fact they may have been wrecked or rendered inoperable the day before.

Marder estimates that over the course of production—from the early meetings deciding the nature and scope of the film, through the round-the-clock, build-Rome-in-a-month crunch that shooting a major film represents—as many as 800 to 1,000 people contributed to the effort. Some of these people were studio employees, some independent contractors who make a living in the movie industry. Other than overseeing the cars, Marder helped coordinate meals, drinks, and restroom facilities for those on location for shooting.

The Fast and The Furious films also relied on car professionals whose skills and facilities were beyond the studio's typical demands and expertise. One of Marder's favorite jobs is finding these outside experts—people who know engines or metal work or upholstery backwards and forwards, inside and out, who can apply their own talents and rally others in their field to assist in the monumental task of preparing dozens of cars for cinema's rigorous, big-screen demands. "I find someone in that world who has all the answers," Marder says. He wins that person's trust, and lets the expert lead Marder to other people and resources he needs to make his part of the production happen.

For another film, *Days of Thunder*, Marder needed help from the NASCAR world. His starting point was Spartanburg, North Carolina. There, he met longtime engine builder Jerry Mason. When Mason introduced him to racing legend Buddy Baker, Marder told Baker, "I'm just a dumb Yankee with a checkbook." Baker busted up and a valuable friendship was formed. That connection allowed Marder to work with NASCAR insiders, who provided fabrication support and cars to meet the film's demands.

It's essential to have a solid relationship with these outside sources because film work is demanding—nearly relentless during the crunch period. Work days are 16 hours long once shooting starts, and the cars get worked on around the clock to keep them looking and running right. When Marder gets an upholstery shop to work on film cars, for example, its employees need to run just as hard as the industry regulars. The job pays well, but the hours are long and the pace daunting. Marder makes sure the car people he brings in understand the situation and are satisfied with their arrangement. "The deal is only good for me if it's good for you," he tells them. For 32 years he has secured local expertise to further major film projects in locations around the world.

As transportation coordinator for *The Fast and the Furious* and *2 Fast 2 Furious*, David Marder had a big job—keeping track of where all the cars being used in filming were, whether in the warehouse lot or being worked on, and making sure they made it on set on time. *Craig Lieberman*

His success comes from an intuitive sense about people, backed by a lot of experience doing his job. "Experience is the best teacher," Marder says. Another ingredient for success in the film business is the ability to change direction quickly, even totally, and not worry about it. Getting a film onto the big screen involves planning and creativity—two unrelated endeavors. A director might see a way to improve a scene days before, or during, shooting that abandons the initial plan and requires an instantaneous new one. Film professionals like Marder switch course without missing a beat. It's the only way to keep things moving forward.

For *2 Fast 2 Furious*, Marder's team rented a 100,000-square-foot warehouse in Miami to store and work on the film's cars. Marder also took over a Miami car dealer's body shop, where mechanics, painters, and auto body experts worked through the night painting, straightening panels and frames, and making any other repairs necessary to get the cars back on the set the following day. Marder also oversaw initial delivery of the cars, which were built in Los Angeles then shipped to Miami on 20-plus car carriers. Another five carriers were in full-time use throughout the production, moving cars between storage, the repair shop, and the main unit (shooting the actors) and second unit (shooting stunts).

Even with these resources, unforeseen challenges came up. At one point during shooting, three of the four cars the studio built were wrecked and the director and second unit director both wanted the remaining car for shooting. Marder's team hauled the remaining car back and forth between the two units as best they could, and the second unit director worked with a different car in the interim. Marder likes to have five examples of each vehicle, but the budget doesn't always allow it.

Early on in a film's production, Marder goes on "tech scouts" with the director. The director describes what he envisions in his mind, while Marder carefully processes what he sees with his eyes. As the months unfold, Marder will be a key player in transforming the director's vision into reality. The transformation will require millions of dollars, hundreds of people, dozens of props, and some plain dealing with knowledgeable folks in the real world Hollywood re-imagines for the screen. It is an intense, at times, grueling journey—one Marder loves to take.

During filming of *2 Fast 2 Furious*, Marder rented a 100,000-square-foot warehouse in Miami to store and work on the film's cars. *Craig Lieberman*

PART 2
2 FAST 2 FURIOUS
(2003)

1999 NISSAN SKYLINE GT-R R34

DRIVEN BY BRIAN O'CONNER (PLAYED BY PAUL WALKER)

>> Since the tuner street racing scene features some of the most spectacular cars on the road—both in looks and performance—getting the best cars for *The Fast and the Furious* films was essential. The powerful and advanced Nissan Skyline GT-R, with its four-wheel steering, was an obvious insider's choice.

Yet the GT-R posed a challenge because the car was not available for sale in the United States. The right-hand drive GT-R and its duplicates tricked out for *2 Fast 2 Furious* had to be imported from Japan just for the film. Although that involved paperwork and the usual risks of shipping delays, damage, and delivery errors, the cars arrived in time to be modified and used in the film.

Another hurdle the filmmakers faced was the all-wheel drive GT-R's tremendous grip, which is safe but not so cinematic. To get a more on-the-edge look, producers disconnected the front driveshaft, allowing Walker and the stunt drivers to spin the rear wheels and kick out the tail for more colorful footage.

When we met Brian O'Conner in *The Fast and the Furious*, he was an undercover cop with no experience in the street racing scene. He knew pursuit driving and eluded other police in a bid to befriend Dom Toretto, but he was not a racer. When *2 Fast 2 Furious* starts, that all has changed. Brian has aquired and tuned his Skyline, and he funded his trip to Miami by winning races along the way. The GT-R is now fully tricked out and painted a classic sliver with smoky blue stripes evocative of the AC Cobras that battled Corvettes on racetracks around the country in the 1960s.

In the first scene of the film, Brian takes a call from his friend and race promoter Tej about subbing into a four-car race for a driver who couldn't make it. O'Conner flashing over Miami's night streets with his Skyline casting an electric-blue glow from its in-car and under-car neon lighting is classic hero-going-to-fight imagery. In an instant, we know this is one of the most formidable cars and drivers on the road. That's the look director John Singleton was after.

The Skyline's role is sweet but short. Brian bests his adversaries Slap Jack in a turbo Supra, Orange Julius in a twin-turbo RX-7, and Suki in a Honda S2000 roadster. He takes Slap Jack in the final stretch, leap-frogging him with a double nitrous shot as both cars launch over a partially raised drawbridge—a stunt Tej put together to make this a memorable race. The stunt drivers performed this scene by driving the Supra and GT-R off a 60-foot long ramp (with the S2000 leaving the same ramp by remote control). The landing from this jump broke the Skyline's oil

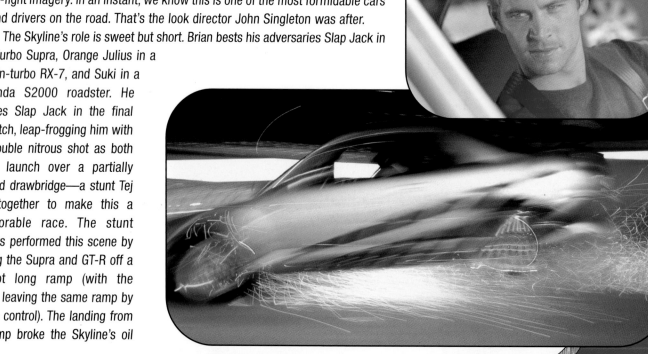

pan and blew out all four tires. But the car crews, which worked round the clock during shooting, got the jumped car back into the lineup in two days.

A big difference between John Singleton's *2 Fast 2 Furious* and the first film is that Singleton wanted to film the stars at the wheel. For many stunts, this was impractical, but Singleton had the principal actors go to performance driving school and showed his stars doing their own driving where it could be done safely. Paul Walker (who owns his own high-performance Skyline in real life) is a highly skilled driver and was at the wheel for some cool shots. At the end of the four-car race, for example, the Skyline passes through a gap in the crowd and slides sideways to a stop. Walker was driving for that footage, which Singleton highlighted by holding the shot and moving into a close-up shot with a steadicam as soon as the car stopped moving.

As cool—and fast—as the Skyline was, it leaves the story after the four-car race when police, using a special high-voltage dart, shut down the car's electrical system as O'Conner tries to bolt away. They've targeted O'Conner because they want him to go undercover again. He's a fugitive at the start of the film, but his captors offer to drop all charges if he'll help them. It's a deal he can't pass up—especially since it means more of the high-speed driving he has come to crave.

Many *2 Fast 2 Furious* fans thought the electric dart was real technology. While the idea seems possible enough, there is no system like this in use by law enforcement. The problems with such a system may be in ensuring that only the car's electrical system, and not its occupants, gets zapped and that the high-voltage jolt doesn't blow the fuel tank. Will such a device appear in the future? Maybe. But for every patrolman eager for such a law-enforcement tool, there's a plaintiff's lawyer ready to add "dart-related injuries" to his yellow pages ad.

While tuners and street racers needed no introduction to the Skyline GT-R, the U.S. auto market did, as Nissan did not export the model to the United States. Because of the car's domestic unavailability, finding doubles became a challenge. John Wiser, one of the transportation gurus on the film, worked with a connection in England to help secure the GT-R stable.

Most challengers see this view of the GT-R only briefly, at the starting line. As O'Conner pulls up to enter the four-car race at the start of the film, his car "snorts" nitrous oxide vapor into the air, like a bull. While the effect makes the car look more threatening, it serves a more practical purpose too: purging the nitrous lines to remove air bubbles for maximum efficiency.

ENGINE:
Twin-turbocharged, 2.6-liter DOHC, 24-valve RB26DETT straight six; Nitrous Express in-car nitrous system, intercooler, and bracketry; K&N Filter ram air upgrade kit

BODY MODS:
C-West/MotoRex body kit; Flexivity rear wing

SUSPENSION MODS:
Goldline lowering springs; JIC Magic-supplied adjustable shocks

INTERIOR:
Sparco seats, steering wheel, and harnesses; APC in-car fire extinguisher; HKS in-dash gauges

SPECIALTY MODS:
Street Glow under-car neon

AUDIO/VIDEO:
Clarion in-dash TV, in-dash head unit; JBL speakers; Infinity amplifiers; Passport radar detectors; MoTeC in-dash LCD data-logging steering wheel

WHEELS:
HRE 446 19-inch

TIRES:
Toyo Proxes

PAINT COLOR:
House of Kolor Platinum Pearl

DOUBLES CONSTRUCTED:
4

This behind-the-scenes GT-R shot shows the car about as innocuous as it gets. Body, graphics, and paint experts will soon transform it into a star car. In the background with its tailgate up is another star car under prep: Slap Jack's Supra.

The body kit's new nose piece improves the front end's look, replacing the squarish single opening below the turn signal lamp with a pair of air passages that complement the curve of the front spoiler.

Under-car lighting is not for everyone, but it gave the already amazing GT-R even more presence. The problem with a car so fast and so noticeable is that every eye in the law enforcement community can lock onto it.

The GT-R picture car fitted with specialty body kit, wheels, rear wing, and full graphics. If you can find a hotter looking car, buy it.

1993 MAZDA RX-7

DRIVEN BY ORANGE JULIUS (PLAYED BY AMAURY NOLASCO)

>> The cars in *The Fast and the Furious* were driven hard and sustained some damage during filming. Those that were demolished, such as the Dodge Charger at the end of the film, sat around as wrecks until they were finally disposed of. Many of the running cars the studio had purchased for the film were simply warehoused after shooting was complete. Among these cars were several RX-7s that had been driven by Vin Diesel's character, Dom Toretto. They would make a repeat appearance in *2 Fast 2 Furious*.

The third-generation twin-turbocharged rotary-engined RX-7 was a Corvette killer when it appeared in 1993. This car was fast—one of the fastest stock vehicles used in the first film. Because of the car's reputation on the street, and the fact that the studio had a few on hand, it was a natural for the second film as well. But the cars could not bear a resemblance to Toretto's machine—any more than a human star from the first film could show up in the second with a different name.

Making Orange Julius' car a completely fresh ride required a full makeover. The first round of body kits from Veilside were stripped off and replaced with very different ones from Versus. The new fiberglass pieces changed the nose, wheel arches, and door sills. The GT rear wing was removed for a clean finish to the back end, and flip-up headlights like a stock RX-7's were fitted up front (in place of the fixed headlights with clear covers used in *The Fast and the Furious*). Different wheels and a bright orange paint job with yellow and orange designs and digital lettering rounded out the new look. The final product looked lean, mean, and fast. And it was.

In the film, Orange Julius, played by Amaury Nolasco, talks smack to Suki in her S2000 prior to a race that also includes Slap Jack in his Supra. They're missing a fourth, and Tej says their race is no go if they can't come up with one. When they explain that the man they were counting on had to work graveyard shift, Tej lines up his own replacement: Brian O'Conner in his fly silver and blue Skyline GT-R.

Even among fast company, the RX-7 has race car looks—wide and low and aerodynamic. With Orange Julius leaning on the hood of the car prior to the race, and the orange neon under-car lighting blending with the bright paint, the front air dam looks like it's almost touching the ground. Still when O'Conner suggests raising the bet $500—"let's kick it a nickle"—Julius doesn't want to play. O'Conner pushes him, though, and tells him to ask people to clear out so he can leave, and Julius throws down. Thirty-five hundred bucks apiece.

Julius doesn't get the drop, though. The Supra and the Skyline get ahead of him and he battles Suki for third. She gets by him in a late turn and he does a sliding stop rather than pitch his ride over the drawbridge Tej has partially raised. The RX-7 returns in the big scramble at the end of the film when O'Conner and Roman Pearce, played by Tyrese Gibson, are trying to shake virtually every cop car in south Florida off their tails. Like O'Conner's Evo and Pearce's Mitsubishi Spyder, the RX-7 makes it to "The End" of *2 Fast 2 Furious* in one piece.

1993 MAZDA RX-7 SPECIFICATIONS

ENGINE:
Stock sequentially turbocharged 13B twin rotor

BODY MODS:
Versus Motorsports body kit; J-Spec hood; CAT2 fog lights

SPECIALTY MODS:
Street Glow under-car neon

WHEELS:
RO_JA 18x7-inch front, 18x8-inch rear

TIRES:
Toyo T1-S 235/40/ZR18 front, 255/35/ZR18 rear

SUSPENSION MODS:
None

The studio didn't have all the cars on hand—original plus duplicates—that it needed to begin shooting. A couple stock versions were purchased from private owners, then built up like Orange Julius's picture car. This one, along with the silver car in the background, has lost its stock nose in preparation for the front body kit piece.

PAINT COLOR:
House of Kolor Ultra Orange

DOUBLES CONSTRUCTED:
4

The studio held onto many of the cars from the first film. Orange Julius's RX-7 was built from Dom Toretto's car, though the exterior was much revised—with new wheels, paint, graphics, body kit, and removed wing—to give it a fresh look.

1993 TOYOTA SUPRA TURBO

DRIVEN BY SLAP JACK (PLAYED BY MICHAEL EALY)

>> One of the most powerful cars on the set for *2 Fast 2 Furious* was Slap Jack's 1993 turbo Supra. This car, with a very sweet clear, louvered hood panel and afro-comb graphic down the side, did not come to the production in such fine form. In fact, this car was pulled from the Universal Studios warehouse—one of the cars done up as Brian O'Conner's second ride (after his green Eclipse gets shot up and explodes) in the first film.

Builder Eddie Paul and his crew did a first-rate job modifying the car to give it a completely fresh look for *2 Fast 2 Furious*. The mods included different body kits, a different hood, a different paint color, different graphics, and the replacement of the ARP GT2-Series alloy wing with a Versus wing in body color. These cars were used hard in the first film and were not perfectly straight when put into storage. As a result, all of the new body kits had to be customized to fit seamlessly for the second film.

In *2 Fast 2 Furious*, the Supra belongs to Slap Jack, played by Michael Ealy. We meet Slap Jack in the opening race. Like the first dash in *The Fast and the Furious*, this contest involves four cars. This time, however, it is not a one-way race—director John Singleton wanted to up the ante and make this contest even more exciting. Instead, it's a circuit of (illegally) closed streets, with the drivers running a varied course of straightaways and turns and returning to the original starting point.

Slap Jack gets out first in his Supra, leading O'Conner until he makes a wide turn and O'Conner cuts inside for the lead. Yet staying out front is not Slap Jack's—or any of the racers'—only problem. Race organizer Tej has his cohorts partially raise a drawbridge over the river. Slap Jack decides to take it with a shot of nitrous. O'Conner hits a double shot and sails over him as both cars jump. Suki juices up with nitrous, but Orange Julius slides his twin-turbo RX-7 to a stop and spares it the leap. On impact, Slap Jack loses control and slams the Supra into the base of a billboard hard enough to knock the rear body kit loose. Singleton and his crew spent an entire week of evenings shooting this one race.

These turbo Supras were fast cars and well up to the speeds directors Rob Cohen and John Singleton wanted for the two films. The picture car was especially dressed up with lots of performance goodies from GReddy. To avoid replicating those costs for each of the cars used in the film, builder Eddie Paul got a clear top-down photograph of the built-up engine, had the photograph blown up to actual engine size, and then mounted it to a piece of poster board. He then installed this board below the Lexan panel in each of the cars to produce the same look as the car with the tricked-out engine. While movie cameras capture wonderful imagery and allow a very unique form of story-telling, they are easy to fool. On film, these mocked-up photographs looked identical to the genuine engine, sparing Singleton's production the cost of several equally customized powerplants.

In the film, Slap Jack repairs the damage and has the car back in tip-top condition for the scene with O'Conner and Pearce as they flee massive police pursuit during their mission to deliver Carter Verone's drug money to him before he blows town. In this scene, the principal Supra movie car was putting out more than 650 horsepower. Given the car's small size and relatively light weight, this type of power makes for exhilarating performance—from 0–60 in just over 4 seconds, with a top speed of over 175 miles per hour.

One of Slap Jack's Supras developed from Brian O'Conner's second car in *The Fast and the Furious* was initially owned by technical advisor Craig Lieberman. He estimates that the car came to the production with 500 horsepower at the wheels and didn't shed any during its buildup for the camera. These were fast cars.

Audio and video equipment fills the Supra's hatch, along with a pair of NOS nitrous oxide bottles.

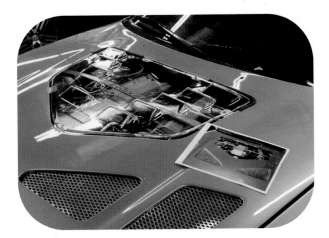

Like the RX-7s, the Supras were revamped versions from the first film, totally restyled for a fresh look. The *2 Fast 2 Furious* Supra's look was brainstormed at Eddie Paul's El Segundo shop. Paul used his vacuum-molding machine to form the distinctive louvered Lexan hood panel.

ENGINE:
3-liter, DOHC, 24-valve 2JZ-GTE inline six; GReddy T-88 single turbo; Power Extreme exhaust, intercooler, polished intake manifold, fuel rail, fuel injector, and clutch upgrades; polished valve cover; custom oil fill cap; Hose Techniques colored hoses; Nitrous Express nitrous system

BODY MODS:
Versus Motorsports wide body kit, rear wing, and hood; FET/Catz HID lights; custom Lexan clear, louvered hood panel

SPECIALTY MODS:
Street Glow under-car neon lighting

WHEELS:
OZ SuperLeggera 19x8.5-inch front, 19x10-inch rear

TIRES:
Toyo T1-S 245/35/ZR19 front, 275/30/ZR19 rear

SUSPENSION MODS:
GReddy strut tower bar

PAINT COLOR:
House of Kolor Gold

DOUBLES CONSTRUCTED:
4

The engine in the picture car was fully dressed and modified to look like heaven and go like hell. The others looked identical on film through a little cinematic sleight of hand: a high-resolution photo of the true engine mounted under the Lexan hood panel.

A pair of Slap Jack's and Suki's rides prior to filming. By the time they're done, the original and duplicates of each car will be indistinguishable. Keeping the cars identical gets trickier once they start sustaining scratches, dings, and worse during shooting.

Painting one car properly takes careful surface preparation, masking, and spray technique. The crew building *The Fast and the Furious* cars had to paint dozens of cars with finishes that would look identical and last—no peeling or flaking off in the hot sun and or at high speeds. Here a Supra gets a fresh coat of gold.

Director John Singleton coordinated each car's design with the character driving it. The afro comb graphic marked the side of Slap Jack's Supra. The graphic is also styled and placed to create a sense of speed.

2000 HONDA S2000

DRIVEN BY SUKI (PLAYED BY DEVON AOKI)

>> Director John Singleton wanted the cars in *2 Fast 2 Furious* to be totally different from those in the first movie. He also wanted a strong connection between the car star and the human star driving it. This vision accounts for the afro-comb graphic that personalizes Slap Jack's Supra and also for the arresting airbrush designs that bedeck Suki's hot-pink Honda.

Singleton drew upon many influences for his film's look, including Japanese anime. The airbrushed girl down the sides of Suki's ride evokes this imagery, with a hint of elfin warrior mixed in. During the first race, Suki's dash-mounted monitor even displays an anime girl who growls with her at the competition.

To handle all the road-race footage and allow for repairs and bodywork, Singleton and his team used four S2000s, all painted with a design similar enough that it would not be possible to tell one car from another when different vehicles were used in different segments. California-based artist Noah, of Noah Fine Art, was able to airbrush the same anime girl, swirl, and bubble design on each Honda.

Replicating the paint job was not the only problem. Once the cars started driving and sustaining damage—as when Suki, played by Devon Aoki, nudges Orange Julius' RX-7 from the back during the four-car race—the damage had to be the same on any other Honda used in that portion of story footage. Even hitting a traffic cone at high speed can make a meaningful dent or crack in a car's bodywork. Technicians were busy as both creators and destroyers, repairing damage that interfered with any car's operation or safety and reproducing filmed cosmetic damage on duplicate cars subbed in.

Suki's car is one of three that go over the partially raised drawbridge at the end of the initial race. The Honda posed a special challenge for this stunt. O'Conner's Skyline and Slap Jack's Supra make the jump first in the film, but both of those cars are coupes. Their roofs shielded protective gear rigged for the stunt drivers to lessen the force of the impact (each driver wore a harness attached to the roll cage with cords). This suspension system reduced the amount of the stuntman's weight effectively slamming into the ground when the car landed. Without it, the force of the landing would be comparable to a stunt driver jumping off the top of the ramp and landing on his backside on the street below. Such a force could crush vertebrae and leave a stunt professional permanently injured. Even with this safety rigging, the Skyline's stunt driver was almost knocked out when that car slammed down into the pavement on landing. Nobody said their job was easy.

Because Suki's Honda had no roof, there was no way to provide a stunt driver in that car with adequate crash protection for a major jump. Instead technicians rigged one of the cars for remote-control operation. The operator followed in a chase car, providing gas, brake, and steering inputs as if the Honda were a more typical remote-control toy. The gearbox was left in second and the operator had a switch to engage the clutch on launch. Even in this limited configuration, the powerful Honda was able to do burnouts and reach 50 miles per hour. The Honda hit the jump faster than the Skyline and Supra, and landed more nose-down—an impact that broke off the bodywork forward of the radiator and produced a shower of sparks that looked great in the final cut. Still, the little Honda was tough enough that the crew patched it up and put it back into service after the jump.

Suki's supercharged Honda S2000 was a serious performer. The paint job is feminine in the extreme, yet one of the nicest in the film, with custom airbrushing by Noah of Noah Fine Art, Costa Mesa, California.

The custom anime girl, bubbles, and swirls mark every body panel. Keen observers will note that in this shot the pink, double-domed panel covering the convertible top and aligning with each headrest is not in place.

The custom bodywork on Suki's car elongated the nose and made it somewhat pointier, and added wider fender flares, hood bulges, and the panel behind the headrests. The overall effect is a more detailed body that hints at high performance.

ENGINE:
2-liter, aluminum-alloy, DOHC F20C1 inline 4-cylinder; Comptech supercharger system with Paxton Novi 1000; Toucan Industries exhaust; Ractive chrome tip (non-functioning, rigged to shoot flames for filming)

BODY MODS:
Veilside Millenium body kit

INTERIOR:
Sparco seats, steering wheel, and harness; A'PEXi tach, boost, EGT, and temperature gauges; Passport radar detector; APC fire extinguisher; Street Glow in-car neon lighting

SPECIALTY MODS:
Street Glow under-car neon lighting

WHEELS:
Motegi Racing 18x7.5-inch front, 18x8-inch rear

TIRES:
Toyo T1-S 225/35/ZR18 front, 265/35/ZR18 rear

SUSPENSION MODS:
Stock

PAINT COLOR:
House of Kolor NE-514 Pink

DOUBLES CONSTRUCTED:
3

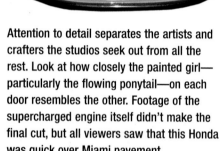

Attention to detail separates the artists and crafters the studios seek out from all the rest. Look at how closely the painted girl—particularly the flowing ponytail—on each door resembles the other. Footage of the supercharged engine itself didn't make the final cut, but all viewers saw that this Honda was quick over Miami pavement.

This car's interior is partially completed, with dash-mounted gauge and video screen, but more pink will come—to the door panels, seats, and shifter boot—before it's ready for the camera.

Clean alloy struts, bolted from within the trunk, support a body-colored wing, which has been treated like all body panels to custom airbrush details.

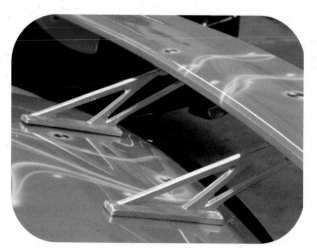

The elfin warrior on the doors suits Suki's character—small but strong and without fear. Actress Devon Aoki was a convincing racer, even though she had never driven a car before joining the cast.

Although larger scale, the Honda's controls were not much different from a toy car's, providing radio control for acceleration, turning, and braking. The transmission was left in second gear, which in the S2000 allowed adequate speed for the bridge jump.

This is not Hollywood's shortest stunt driver. The real driver is in another car testing out this Honda's remote controls. Because the S2000 is topless and therefore unable to protect a stunt driver with a suspension harness, the Honda had to be jumped empty—that is, via remote control.

2002 MITSUBISHI EVO VII

DRIVEN BY BRIAN O'CONNER (PLAYED BY PAUL WALKER)

>> At the end of *The Fast and the Furious*, O'Conner helps Dom Toretto chase down thugs who have shot and killed one of Toretto's de facto family members, Jesse. O'Conner then races Dom for a moment's peace from their enveloping troubles. Toretto wrecks badly, and as the sirens wail to investigate this street race gone bad, O'Conner sets his outlaw friend free—in his own car.

O'Conner flees himself, to Miami, picking up a Skyline GT-R along the way and building it into the supreme street racer on the local scene. But the law has caught up with him and the Skyline goes down in a police chase, shot with a high-voltage dart, after O'Conner wins a four-case race at the start of *2 Fast 2 Furious*.

His replacement for the Skyline is a Mitsubishi Evolution (Evo) VII, one of the most dangerous sedans a stoplight-to-stoplight racer could make the mistake of challenging. With 276 stock horsepower in a body that weighs as much as a tennis-ball can, the Evo can eat up pavement. (Producers left the all-wheel drive Evo turning all four meats.) It is only a few tenths of a second behind a legendary AC Shelby 427 Cobra going 0–60, with over 30 years' worth of improved automotive technology to draw on once turned loose on the street. A complication of that technology is that the cops who have forced O'Conner back behind a badge to help them with their case against criminal Carter Verone have hardwired the Evo with a tracking device. They don't want O'Conner driving into the sunset again, mission unaccomplished.

Stunt drivers and actor Paul Walker got to blur a lot of scenery at the wheel of the Evo in *2 Fast 2 Furious*. The first good airing out for the VII is an audition run among many would-be drivers for Verone. O'Conner and Pearce challenge a handful of other lead-foots in some formidable machinery of their own. The object is simple: race to an alleged impound lot miles away and recover a package from Verone's Ferrari.

For this scene, Singleton's crew got to race and shoot the cars on sections of Interstate 95 around Miami that were closed for filming. O'Conner and Pearce led the band of road rockets that included a Yenko Camaro, Hemi Challenger, Saleen Mustang, Corvette, Viper, and BMW M3.

This chase involved more than speed. O'Conner, in the Evo, and Pearce, in a Mitsubishi Spyder, divide a pair of semis before the drivers get wise. When a Saleen Mustang pilot tries to follow, the semis are narrowing the gap. The Mustang bumps the trucks' tires and spins, winding up in front of a trailer's many rear axles. They push the car for a short way before climbing and crushing it. (Don't worry. It wasn't a real Saleen used for the stunt, but a V-6 Mustang dressed up to match.) The Corvette then plows into the wrecked Mustang in a collision that was unplanned. The stunt driver was not hurt, however, so filmmakers cut in a shot of the actor-driver trying a panic stop and kept the footage.

O'Conner and Pearce compete between themselves too, each trying to prove himself against his one-time best friend. O'Conner wins this contest with a 180-degree handbrake spin, after which he leads Pearce backward, looking eye to eye. Actor Paul Walker, the most skillful driver in the cast, actually completed that 180-degree spin on the Florida highway.

Walker and the stunt drivers get to push the Evo hard in two other big driving scenes. First is an out-and-back race for pink slips with the drivers of the Yenko Camaro and Hemi Challenger. O'Conner and Pearce are outgunned on horsepower, but O'Conner buys time by playing chicken until the Camaro driver veers wide, skids out, and loses time. The car also is featured in the final scene when dozens of patrol cars pursue the Evo and Spyder through the Miami area as O'Conner and Pearce try to deliver six bags of cash to Verone while also fulfilling their undercover assignment to help bring him down. Both cars escape undemolished as police apprehend stand-ins Tej and Suki after O'Conner and Pearce swap rides for the Yenko and Hemi. The Yenko takes top stunt honors after the car jumps onto the back of Verone's fleeing yacht.

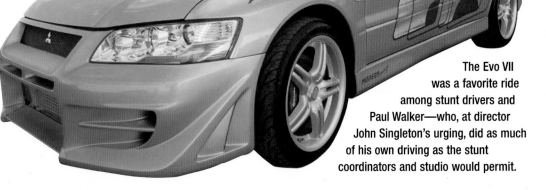

The Evo VII was a favorite ride among stunt drivers and Paul Walker—who, at director John Singleton's urging, did as much of his own driving as the stunt coordinators and studio would permit.

According to technical advisor Craig Lieberman, Mitsubishi wanted the film's Evo VIIs modified to use Evo VIII–style taillights because the company had no plans to sell the VII in the United States. To make the change, Eddie Paul and his crew worked an entire weekend straight.

While the new taillights resembled the Evo VIII's, with a prominent circular lens for each bulb rather than the VII's full-colored lens, the assemblies were narrower than the opening. Paul had to fabricate the lip to fill what would otherwise have been a gap between the quarter panel and the taillight's outer edge.

ENGINE:
Turbocharged, 2-liter, DOHC, 16-valve 4G63 inline 4-cylinder with nitrous system

BODY MODS:
DAMD body kit; ARC rear wing; Genera TYC custom-fabricated taillights

SPECIALTY MODS:
Street Glow under-car neon lighting

WHEELS:
Motegi Racing

TIRES:
Toyo T1-S 235/45/ZR17

SUSPENSION MODS:
Stiffer springs and aftermarket shocks

PAINT COLOR:
House of Kolor Lime Gold

DOUBLES CONSTRUCTED:
4

The body kit didn't change the front end too much. Perhaps the most prominent change was the steel-colored mesh across the air openings as opposed to the blacked-out stock look.

The body kit's front air dam had a different side vent from the stock version, and the Mitsubishi wheels would go before the car was done. No need to change much on an Evo, though, as the manufacturer had already punched it up to a much higher level than a typical import sedan.

Wing on, graphics pending. When Mitsubishi struck its deal with the studio to feature the Evo VII, it had to divert a few cars destined for a rally team to meet the film's schedule.

The finished product looks like a rally car—what Mitsubishi built it to be, though not quite like this. The Evo's rally breeding gave the production crew both speed and ruggedness—desirable qualities when you're shooting a car movie 16 hours a day.

2001 MITSUBISHI ECLIPSE SPYDER

DRIVEN BY ROMAN PEARCE (PLAYED BY TYRESE GIBSON)

>> Along with Brian O'Conner's Evo VII, Roman Pearce's Mitsubishi Eclipse Spyder is one of the main star cars in *2 Fast 2 Furious*. Pearce joins O'Conner in plenty of flat-out driving, including a race for pink slips against a Yenko Camaro and Hemi Challenger, a less formal scramble to secure a package from Verone's Ferrari, and a final run from a swarm of police cruisers when it all goes down at the end of the film.

The Spyder and its doubles were modified twice for the film. The initial paint job didn't appeal to actor Tyrese Gibson, who played Pearce. That design featured a more obvious spiderweb pattern down the sides of the car, with a solid purple hood. The car also had a bright yellow interior, different wheels, and a subtler rear spoiler.

Tyrese helped guide the restyle, creating a more eye-catching car, with an intricate silver and purple web of small squares and subtle bending lines laid over the hood, wrapping across the tops of the doors onto the rear quarter panel. A swooshing Z-like design emerged from the top and back of the front wheel well and swept across the door fading into the top of the quarter panel and the rear wheel well. Gibson also selected new polished-alloy wheels to complement the design.

The yellow interior, customized and carefully installed, had to be swapped out, too. While it may have reflected a street-racer's desire for a little attention, it also reflected a lot of sunlight onto the front windshield, making it difficult for the driver to see in the intense Miami rays. Car builder Eddie Paul and his crew fitted a wide body kit and rear wing, plus custom taillights to further set the Spyder apart. Like the Evo, the Spyder gets out alive, finishing the film without suffering a crash, flipover, fire, or hailstorm of bullets.

Roman Pearce enters the scene in *2 Fast 2 Furious* in a demolition derby car. From there, he upgrades to a fly Eclipse Spyder, which he uses with O'Conner (driving his Evo VII) to beat a Camaro and Dodge Challenger for pink slips. Not a bad run of cars.

This custom interior was quite distinctive—too much so, in fact. What drivers encountered may well explain why we don't see a lot of bright yellow dashboards in custom cars: the glare it produced off the inside of the windshield was a real distraction. Even at the driver's door's oblique angle, the yellow shows clearly in the side window glass.

ENGINE:
Stock 200-horsepower, 24-valve, 3-liter V-6

BODY MODS:
Shine Street wide body kit and rear wing; APC carbon fiber hood; Genera/TYC Euro taillights

SUSPENSION:
Stock

INTERIOR:
Sparco seats; V-Racing steering wheel and shift knob; APC gauges; Street-Glow in-car neon lighting

AUDIO/VIDEO:
Rockford Fosgate amps and speakers; Panasonic in-dash head unit and in-dash television; Myron Davis auxiliary TVs

WHEELS:
Lowenhart BR-5

TIRES:
BF Goodrich 245/35/ZR20

PAINT COLOR:
House of Kolor Purple with silver web graphic

DOUBLES CONSTRUCTED:
4

The first paint job failed to make it to the silver screen. The reason: actor Tyrese Gibson didn't like it. He didn't think much of the rims either, so they were kicked off the film.

A Shine Street body kit and wing give Pearce's Spyder a jet-like aerodynamic profile.

This paint job is more what actor Tyrese Gibson had in mind. The Spyder, as it appears in the film, has coordinated paint and interior colors, much cooler wheels, and a more refined "spider web" design.

Tyrese looks at home in the Spyder he helped restyle. This car isn't totally done, though. The sharp-eyed observer will notice that the wheels on this car are not the polished Lowenhart rims that appear on screen.

2000 ACURA NSX

DRIVEN BY TEJ (PLAYED BY CHRIS "LUDACRIS" BRIDGES)

>> Tej, played by singer Chris "Ludacris" Bridges, is the main race promoter in *2 Fast 2 Furious*. He has a garage and shop on the Miami River and his spread is a primary gathering point for street racers and beautiful women. Except for a rabbit run he and Suki make at the end of the film to lure police away from O'Conner and Pearce, who have switched cars, we don't see Tej race. His role is at the starting line, setting the rules and making sure the crowd sees a thrilling display of skill.

But as a man into the tuner and wrenching scene, Tej has some hot cars. These include his dazzling brown and gold Acura NSX, whose paint design mimics a Louis Vuitton purse—something the ladies can appreciate. Instead of LV, however, the two interlocked letters on Tej's car are TJ. Along with gorgeous women and other fine cars, the NSX fills out the background when Brian and Roman Pearce come to seek lodging for Pearce, whom Tej says can crash in his houseboat.

2 Fast 2 Furious director John Singleton likes Steven Spielberg's philosophy of composing interesting shots so the audience has plenty to look at, and that's part of the reason Tej's NSX is prime eye candy. There's also a four-door Dodge Ram pickup in the same houseboat scene that features the gold and brown Luis Vuitton/Tej paint pattern.

The film's NSXs, which perform well in stock trim, were not modified for performance. Yet the bodies saw additional work beyond the paint. To distinguish this star car from others of the same model, the builders fitted a set of razor-back scoops starting on the roof, flowing down the back of the car like an alligator's scales. Fabricator Eddie Paul and his crew mocked up scoops from cardboard for fit, then shaped them in wood, and finally in ABS plastic on a vacuum-forming machine. The finished pieces created a hungry air-intake look for feeding a cool, stiff breeze into the engine compartment. A body kit was also fitted to enhance the car's ground-hugging stance. A triple-blade alloy wing on the

rear and low-profile, five-spoke polished alloy wheels completed the high-performance look with style.

Ludacris had not acted in a film before, but had plenty of experience in front of audiences as a rapper. Because the tuner scene blends high-performance engines and high-tech audio and video systems, music is an important part of the culture. Hip-hop star Ja Rule played a small role in *The Fast and the Furious* and Ludacris carried on that tradition in the second film. Co-star Tyrese Gibson, who plays O'Conner's childhood buddy Pearce, is also a part of the music scene. Gibson is an R&B singer who cut his first album, which went platinum, at age 19.

2000 ACURA NSX SPECIFICATIONS

ENGINE:
Stock 290-horsepower, 3.2-liter,
24-valve V-6

BODY MODS:
Custom scoop and body kit

INTERIOR:
Sparco seats; APC in-car fire extinguisher

SPECIALTY MODS:
None

WHEELS:
Alloy, 16-inch front, 17-inch rear

PAINT COLOR:
House of Kolor Brown and gold, with pattern emulating Louis Vuitton purse design, using letters TJ

DOUBLES CONSTRUCTED:
3

The scoops were originally mocked up in cardboard for dimensions and to ensure that the rear hatch would still open and close with the final items in place. It would have been simpler to ignore the hatch, but at the time Eddie Paul and his crew were building the cars they did not know how much attention each would receive on screen. Since these are car-enthusiast films, attention to detail prevailed in planning the custom scoops.

The "gatorback" scoops going up the hatch on Tej's Acura NSX were one of the cooler custom touches in the *2 Fast 2 Furious* stable. Unfortunately, the scoops did not get much screen time in the final cut. The car appears only briefly outside Tej's riverside garage.

1969 YENKO CAMARO

DRIVEN BY KORPI (PLAYED BY JOHN CENATIEMPO) & BRIAN O'CONNER

>> Using the Yenko Camaro in *2 Fast 2 Furious*, along with the Hemi Challenger R/T, was a nod to the films' viewers who grew up in a different hot rodding and street racing era. Before imports became the most widely available cars for young people to buy, inherit, fix up, and hop up, those roles were filled by American cars. Drag racing and stoplight-to-stoplight contests of an earlier generation were dominated by muscle cars—simple, inexpensively built bodies, chassis, and interiors matched with a big V-8 hunk of iron under the hood. Before turbos and nitrous oxide, the old saying was, "there's no substitute for cubic inches."

Don Yenko was a Pennsylvania car dealer who catered to young drivers looking for that extra level of performance. He would take cars already known for their street power and ramp them up to quarter-mile contender specs by installing Chevy's formidable 427-cubic-inch V-8. Yenkos were rare, fast cars in their time, and today those few remaining cars not blown up or smashed to pieces by a chain of speed freaks command enormous dollars.

The *2 Fast 2 Furious* Yenko is featured in an eight-car scramble to recover a package that villain Carter Verone sends them for as a test to see who will become his driver for an even bigger job. The Camaro gets to flex its muscle on Interstate 95 near Miami, along with O'Conner's Evo, Pearce's Mitsubishi Spyder, plus a Saleen Mustang, Cobra, Corvette, Hemi Challenger, and BMW M3. This big-block Camaro can get up with the best of them.

It becomes O'Conner's—and the Challenger Pearce's—when the two reunited friends beat the Chevy and Dodge in an out-and-back street race for pink slips. It's a race they were losing to the drag-strip giants before O'Conner goes directly at the Yenko's driver, Korpi, and that racer veers, skidding out and losing precious seconds.

The Camaro earns a special role in the film as the car O'Conner and Pearce launch off a pier in a spectacular jump onto Verone's yacht. It's their last chance to catch him before he escapes with Monica, Verone's girlfriend, whom he has discovered is an undercover cop—with eyes for O'Conner. She's dead if O'Conner and Pearce can't stop Verone.

Jumping the Camaro was a stunt with four components. In the first, a lightened car drained of toxic fluids, fitted with a false bottom, and filled with foam is pulled by cable off a jump into the ocean. The initial part of this arc is then matched to another Camaro suspended by a cable over dry asphalt. That car descends into a full-scale, detailed mockup of the top rear portion of Verone's yacht, crashing into it with good speed and sending chunks of yacht, a

ENGINE:
427-cubic-inch L72 pushrod V-8

BODY MODS:
None

SPECIALTY MODS:
None

WHEELS:
Cragar S/S

TIRES:
BF Goodrich Radial T/A

SUSPENSION MODS:
Stock Yenko

PAINT COLOR:
House of Kolor Le Mans Blue

DOUBLES CONSTRUCTED:
4

Year One produced a meticulously detailed replica of a genuine Yenko Camaro, right down to the 427 V-8. This was a very fast car, representing cubic inches in the displacement versus forced-induction battles on screen. O'Conner beat it in his Evo, but only by winning a game of "chicken" with the Yenko's driver.

jet-ski, and other projectiles flying. Paul Walker and Tyrese Gibson were placed in a third car set up in a special-effects studio before a green screen. This car provides the close-ups of O'Conner and Pearce as they sail through the air in this insane automotive leap. Footage of Miami waterways could then be inserted in the editing room to keep the apparent location consistent. The final chunk involved putting the Camaro on the back of a real yacht, carefully and purposely damaged to duplicate the fake one the suspended Camaro crashed into. From this, O'Conner and Pearce emerge to capture Verone with Monica's help.

Don't lament the Yenko Camaro's harsh treatment. No one lets cars like this get destroyed. The jumps and crashes involve duplicate cars and portions of cars rejuvenated from junkyard vehicles for that purpose. Because these films draw hardcore enthusiasts, the studio had a replica Yenko built for closer shots that matched the original right down to the engine.

It's a car . . . it's a plane . . . it's a boat—or on one. The Yenko Camaro covered land, air, and sea in *2 Fast 2 Furious*. The cars used for the stunts were not real Yenkos, or even decent Camaros, but wrecks carefully repaired for bruising stunt duty.

1970 DODGE HEMI CHALLENGER R/T

DRIVEN BY SCOTT DARDEN (PLAYED BY ERIC ETEBARI)
& ROMAN PEARCE

>> The Hemi Challenger joined the Yenko Camaro as a representative of the earlier street racing era when cubic inches ruled. It is featured in the same scenes as the Camaro—the run to the alleged impound lot in a dash villain Carter Verone has staged to find the best drivers for a subsequent job; a pink-slips race with O'Conner and Pearce; and the mad dash at the end of the film, when O'Conner and Pearce have swapped out their Evo and Mitsubishi Spyder for these high-horsepower monsters for the final sprint to Verone with his money and the authorities in tow.

Only one of the Challengers on duty for the film was a true Hemi. The others sported more common Mopar big-block engines, like the 440. The Hemi came to the production with a dual-quad setup on cross-ram manifold, but mechanics swapped it to a single four-barrel during shooting so it would stay in tune during hard runs.

Like the Yenko, the Hemi Challenger is a rare vehicle whose time among collectors has come. A new Hemi Challenger in 1970 was on the order of $4,000. Today these cars routinely command prices well into six figures.

Rest assured, the Challenger that Pearce blows the door off of to eject his passenger in *2 Fast 2 Furious* is not a Hemi.

1970 DODGE HEMI CHALLENGER R/T SPECIFICATIONS

ENGINE:
426-cubic-inch Hemi pushrod V-8 with dual 750-cfm Holley carburetors on cross-ram manifold

BODY MODS:
Stock

SPECIALTY MODS:
None

WHEELS:
Five-spoke grey mags

TIRES:
BF Goodrich

SUSPENSION MODS:
Stock

PAINT COLOR:
House of Kolor Red with black stripe on hood and tail

DOUBLES CONSTRUCTED:
3

The Dodge Hemi Challenger: another throwback to the era when displacement ruled the racing scene. These muscle car classics were included in *The Fast and The Furious* films to remind the younger generation of the first kings of the road.

CRAIG LIEBERMAN

Technical advisor on The Fast and The Furious *and* 2 Fast 2 Furious

Craig Lieberman, former director of the National Import Racing Association and co-founder/creator of NOPI Drag Racing Association, helped bring an authentic look and feel to the cars and racing scenes in *The Fast and the Furious* movies. *Craig Lieberman*

>> *The Fast and the Furious* films were born from an article on street racing, "Racer X," that appeared in the May 1998 issue of *Vibe* magazine. In it, Kenneth Li showcased the energy and enthusiasm behind street racing so well that Universal Studios executives thought the piece could be transformed into a compelling movie. They were right.

But the studio's expertise was in storytelling, not performance automobiles. To present the street racing world with an appropriate degree of authenticity, the studio needed a performance expert immersed in tuner culture. The search led them to Craig Lieberman, former director of the National Import Racing Association and co-founder/creator of NOPI Drag Racing Association.

His finger was on the pulse of the import tuner scene. He knew a lot about L.A.'s most devastating street racing machines, so he helped the studio choose the cars to feature in the first two films. Most of them were modeled on real cars whose owners had spent one to three years building them. In fact, his own Supra, which made about 500 horsepower at the wheels, was the "10-second car" Brian O'Conner gives to Dom Toretto at the end of *The Fast and the Furious*.

Lieberman was also empowered to shop for performance goodies to make the cars move like their real-life counterparts. He then worked closely with studio mechanics, headed by Tim Woods, who wrenched the cars into road-rocket form.

When various members of the media started to deride *The Fast and the Furious* because of its connection to illegal street racing, Lieberman put the issue in perspective by pointing out that street racing is a lot older than the film. In fact, drivers have been going wheel-to-wheel pretty much since the second car (ever) was built, and illegal street racing reflects this inherent drive to be fastest. In ancient times, people raced on foot and in chariots.

As wrangled as police and communities may become over street racing, most acknowledge that the kids behind the wheel are not inherently troublemakers headed for more destructive illegal endeavors. Unlike other unlawful activities, street racing only needs an authorized venue to

For *The Fast and the Furious: Tokyo Drift*, Lieberman provided many of the cars that make only brief appearances in the film, but add to the authenticity of the Japanese form of racing. *Craig Lieberman*

become legal. In fact, in some communities, police and city officials have teamed together to sponsor racetracks or legal street races with a safer competitive environment.

Illegal street racing still occurs and probably always will until the automobile—or people's competitive nature—disappears, yet concerted efforts to address or relocate the problem have had an effect. Lieberman says that today's illegal street races are "more like street raves than races. They are gathering spots for people, most of whom just want to hang out with friends."

While the films didn't spawn street racing culture, they did have an impact on the young men and women who love it. Lieberman notes that while some serious tuners found the cars a bit overdone and dismissed the criminal-activities angle as the movie fiction it was, the films boosted tuner culture by drawing in a new crop of young enthusiasts.

"These new tuners latched onto styling and accessorization cues taken from the movie, especially in places like Europe and Japan," Lieberman says. "There was no shortage of imitators both domestically and abroad."

Likewise, the tuner scene had a major impact on the film. "[*The Fast and the Furious* director] Rob Cohen—and indeed the entire production team, including people like Waldemar Kalinowski [production designer for the film]—were very keen on researching the cars, the people, the magazines—every component of the tuner world. They immersed themselves in the culture from top to bottom, studying street racers, their cars, their events, their habits, everything," Lieberman says.

Lieberman points out that "one of [the production team's] greatest successes was their commitment to authentic sound effects for the cars." Sound technicians took the actual high-performance tuners featured in the films and recorded their engines shrieking and howling under all-out driving

at Agua Dulce Airport, near Palmdale. That authenticity struck a chord with enthusiasts, and no doubt won over a few more folks to Japanese horsepower.

Naturally, not all aspects of a fictionalized movie story are true to reality. What about the mark of prestige from the first film—O'Conner's debt to Dom Toretto of a 10-second car? Is that fast? Lieberman says yes. "A 10-second car back then was quick, for a street car," he adds. "But I should point out that LT1 Camaro and 5-liter Mustang guys were running this quick with light modifications about 10 years ago [and heavily modified big-block muscle cars even before that in the late 1960s]. It was not until about 2001 that you began to see 10-second imports as 'street cars.' Even today, unless you're running a Toyota Supra or a Mazda RX-7 with some pretty serious modifications, only a few of these tuner cars are this quick and still drivable on the street."

Lieberman loves the import tuner scene because of the hard work and passion the racers pour into their cars. "This is a form of expression like any other creative endeavor," he says. "It is, quite simply, all about the process of making art in motion. Their vehicles become canvasses of personalization on which they create images of speed and beauty.

"If you've ever drooled over a car magazine, ever shared a performance stat with a buddy, or ever dreamed about horsepower and chrome, you're one of us."

Left: Among the excellent background cars in the third *The Fast and the Furious* movie is this Skyline GT-R, owned by Signal Auto of Japan. This car was well known on the drag racing circuit, with a 1,000 horsepower engine that has since been detuned to legalize this beast for the street. *Craig Lieberman*

Below: With its carbon-fiber nose, Lamborghini-style "scissor" doors, and high-tech samurai paint job, this custom RX-7 has been a hit on the show circuit. The car, owned by Noel Rollon, also features an elaborate audio/video system, turbo upgrade, and nitrous for all-around full-bore performance. *Craig Lieberman*

PART 3
THE FAST AND THE FURIOUS: TOKYO DRIFT

(2006)

1970 CHEVY MONTE CARLO

DRIVEN BY SEAN BOSWELL (PLAYED BY LUCAS BLACK)

>> As his favorite pastime, cars play a central role in Sean Boswell's life. When we first meet Sean as a bored American high school student in *The Fast and the Furious: Tokyo Drift*, his primary concern and distraction is an old Monte Carlo. The wide rims and tires and the car's throbbing exhaust note suggest there's more to the machine than GM put into it 36 years ago—a lot more, as loudmouth schoolmate, Clay, learns.

The Monte Carlo is a productive focus for Sean's restless energies, but old school or not, its 632-cubic-inch V-8 can get a young man into some trouble, even if the powerplant resides in a car twice his age. Sean's dispute with Clay turns on a casual

The Monte Carlo was built to suit a high school gearhead on a lean budget. It's cosmetically rough, but plenty fast. Picture car coordinator Dennis McCarthy and his crew redid the Chevy to near NASCAR standards with some 700 horsepower on tap.

flirtation with Clay's girlfriend, but there's class warfare here, too. Clay, played by Zachery Ty Bryan, drives the fastest ride his father's money can buy him—a Dodge Viper—and he can't resist talking smack to the working class kid with his hot-rod beater.

The exchange leads to a challenge: a race for pink slips. But there's too much testosterone and horsepower on tap, and both competitors' absolute refusal to lose pushes good judgment, the cars, and the laws of physics too far. Sean's survivor Monte Carlo has run its last race. And so has Sean. For now. On U.S. soil.

Whatever damage Sean and Clay did to their cars, it pales in comparison to the property damage on the site—and the trouble Sean is in. With a growing list of infractions already on record, Sean, played by Lucas Black, has pushed the system too far. His prize from the Monte Carlo/Viper showdown is a ticket to Tokyo, where his military father gets a chance to keep his son on the straight and narrow. Good luck.

Scoop and hood pins warn challengers that there's more going on here than an old car that needs a paint job.

You don't see trunk pins too often—but if you're missing the lock, they're a good idea if you don't want the trunk taking out the back window when you slam on the brakes.

This is no stock small-block Chevy V-8, but a lesson in why it's good to find out what's under another car's hood before you start throwing out challenges. A professional stock car–grade suspension and a Bill Mitchell 632 cubic-inch block made Sean's car really kick it.

ENGINE:

Bill Mitchell 632-cubic-inch big block; Holley 4-barrel carburetor on World Products intake manifold; March Pulley Systems brackets and pulleys; NOS nitrous oxide system; Jaz fuel cell; Earl's Performance Fittings steel braided line and anodized fittings; Hooker headers; Flowmaster dual chamber exhaust; Be Cool radiator; Edelbrock water pump

BODY MODS:

Fiberglass Trends cowl hood; Hella headlights

INTERIOR:

Auto Meter gauges; Covan instrument cluster; Grant three-spoke black steering wheel; Flaming River polished stainless-steel steering column; Beard low-back buckets; Deist seat belts; Matt Sweeney custom-fabricated roll bar and door panels; Hurst vertical floor shifter

SPECIALTY MODS:

Richmond T-10 4-speed transmissiion; Moser 12-bolt A-body rear end

WHEELS:

Cragar 397 Series black, 15x8-inch front, 15x10-inch rear

TIRES:

Goodyear Eagle slicks 27x8-inch front, 27x10-inch rear

SUSPENSION MODS:

Global West front and rear tubular control arms, weight jacks, and year one coil springs; Wilwood disc brakes; Speedway Engineering sway bars; Wenco 1350 extreme performance driveshaft; Quick Ratio steering box with IROC Camaro internals; Matt Sweeney reinforced frame and roll cage; Moser 12-bolt with Moser Spool 4.88 gears; KYB shocks; Lakewood Ladder Bars

PAINT COLOR:

House of Kolor Yellow primer PCL Buff 905 Series

DOUBLES CONSTRUCTED:

11 (1970 and 1971 models were used)

The Monte Carlo takes some hard knocks in the opening stunt sequence. Race tires provided the right look and were up to the punishment.

Sean's Monte Carlo also had a JAZ reinforced fuel cell for safety and a trunk-mounted battery to put some more weight over the drive wheels. Stunt cars get only the amount of fuel needed to do the sequence to further reduce the chance of fire.

Above: The car crew built 11 Monte Carlo duplicates, all identical from 5 to 10 feet away. All were rebuilt to ensure they ran and braked well. Picture cars had glammed up engines, while roll cages and chassis modifications ensured stunt cars held up and protected their drivers.

Right: The race in the unfinished housing development required more than the usual number of duplicates because the car does not survive the stunt sequence.

2001 NISSAN SILVIA S-15

OWNED BY HAN (PLAYED BY SUNG KANG)
DRIVEN BY SEAN BOSWELL

>> Sean's competitive nature and penchant for racing have cost him plenty. He's had to move several times in the States and finally to depart altogether for a new life in Japan. Too bad the plane door didn't close before trouble could follow him aboard. The first woman to catch his eye—like a fish-hook—is the girlfriend of one of Tokyo's most dangerous young men: the Drift King. But fresh in a new country, Sean doesn't even know what drifting is—other than moving from one home to another with no real sense which one will prove permanent.

Unable to keep his mouth shut when the Tokyo auto scene's apex predators cross his path, Sean throws down the gauntlet. He challenges the Drift King, played by Brian Tee. Though he's good with a wrench and sharp at the wheel in a grip-driving contest, Sean hasn't the first clue how to drive for style, tail-end out, rear wheels churning up burnt-rubber clouds. He doesn't even have a car. But another man on the scene—DK's friend and business partner, Han—steps up with a set of keys.

Han, played by Sung Kang, doesn't seem to mind the brash American's inexperience. And he likes his style, enough to lend Sean his own drift machine: a 2002 Nissan Silvia S-15, a car that is up to the challenge. With about

With good power, balance, and rear-wheel drive, the Silvia is a drifting favorite.

250 factory horses, the front-engined rear-drive Silvia is a drifting favorite in Japan. Han's is even better, tricked out with a transplanted RB26DETT turbocharged 2.6-liter straight six from a Nissan Skyline GT-R R34, mated to a Skyline transmission.

Sean's quarter-mile experience is of little use in a drift challenge. He gets brief tips on how to put the Silvia into a drift and then the show is on. The Drift King glides his 350Z effortlessly through the course, unconcerned with any high-speed dashes Sean works up. It's the freewheeling turns that decide the outcome and here Sean has nothing to draw from. It's one thing to hold the tail out once and quite another to link a series of turns in a graceful, smoky slalom, wheels spinning furiously beyond full traction's reach.

The race is a blowout, but in his fierce determination to make a show of it, Sean virtually destroys Han's Silvia—with Han taking it surprisingly well. Sean is now in his debt, and luckily Han needs a pitbull-minded assistant more than he needs a car. He has plenty of resources to build another car whenever he wants one.

The battered S-15 is down but not out entirely. The engine will live on to see another high-revving day pitching a car sideways. But not in the Silvia. Instead, the RB26 engine takes its place under the hood of Sergeant Major Boswell's 1967 Mustang, rejuvenating a car long left idle, for a final showdown against the Drift King.

2001 NISSAN SILVIA S-15 SPECIFICATIONS

ENGINE:
Turbocharged RB26 Skyline GT-R straight six with Earl's Performance steel braided line and anodized fittings

BODY MODS:
C-West body kit; GT rear wing; Ganador mirrors

INTERIOR:
Recaro seat; Takata seat belts; Sparco steering wheel; Auto Meter gauges; custom aluminum instrument cluster; custom fabricated roll bar, door panels, rear firewall, and e-brake handle; blue NOS bottle

SPECIALTY MODIFICATIONS:
Fuel Safe Racing Cells fuel cell

WHEELS:
Volk Racing grey GT-7 No. 0355, 19x8.5-inch front, 19x9.5-inch rear

TIRES:
Toyo Proxes T1R 235/35/ZR19 front, 255/30/ZR19 rear

SUSPENSION MODS:
Stock

PAINT COLOR:
House of Kolor Blue with orange wraparound stripe

DOUBLES CONSTRUCTED:
8 (1999, 2000, and 2001 models were used)

Han's special turbocharged Silvia S-15 makes outstanding power at the rear wheels—essential for keeping the rear end loose to drift.

Aggressive air intakes feed the Silvia's transplanted Skyline powerplant.

2002 NISSAN FAIRLADY 350Z

DRIVEN BY THE DRIFT KING (PLAYED BY BRIAN TEE)

>> As an American military brat in Japan, Sean Boswell has a lot to learn. One of those things is how to drift. Another is not to run afoul of the Drift King, Tokyo's top man in this graceful, yet risky sport. Taking a liking to Neela, DK's girlfriend, of course, is not the way to stay in the Drift King's good graces.

What makes the Drift King dangerous is not just his title and the skills he earned it with. He also has a bad car, where "bad" is so good that no challenger can take his crown. The Drift King's 2003 Nissan 350Z has been carefully tweaked for the precisely controlled chaos drifting represents.

When he gets to Japan, Boswell has a hot temper and a heavy foot, and he's never drifted before. He doesn't know what it feels like to float a car sideways on the edge of a spinout. Nor does he know how to put it into a drift. So it's no surprise that the Drift King has little trouble humiliating him in a Tokyo parking garage when Boswell shoots his mouth off. Sean has a good enough drift car in Han's Silvia S-15, but no experience and no technique.

Doing what the rally drivers or dirt-track racers do in the soft stuff—kicking out the tail—is a lot more difficult on pavement. And that's just the start. While the typical racer seeks traction whenever he can get it, the drifter scoffs at traction, accepting only the least pavement grip necessary to keep the car from flying off the road. Add columns, walls, and parked cars to the venue and you'd better be an expert—a lesson Sean learns too late.

DK's Z stomps on Sean in their first contest, but the second is another story. In the mountains, where Japanese motorsports enthusiasts perfected the art of drifting years ago, DK and the Z push the limits of physics and friction too far. Trying to smash his way to victory, DK puts the ground-hugging Veilside Nissan over the edge and out of the game.

With tinted windows and a dark, crouching profile, the Drift King's 350Z is a mean street predator.

Above and right: All thirteen of the 350Zs built for DK were enhanced to varying degrees. Two cars were built with twin turbochargers and intercoolers to make about 460 horsepower at the rear wheels. The rest had nitrous kits for some extra power on demand.

Drifting is hell on tires, so the car crew worked closely with Toyo to get a rubber compound that would serve filming and stunt needs. Professional drifter Rhys Millen was the lead drift driver on the film.

ENGINE:

3.5-liter VQ35DE V-6 twin turbo with 460 horsepower at the rear

BODY MODS:

Veilside Version 3 wide body kit with carbon fiber hood; Speedway Engineering hood pins; Ghostlight Scarab graphics; Ganador carbon fiber mirrors

INTERIOR:

Sparco Evo L black racing seats, seat belts, and steering wheel; Safety 21 roll cage

SPECIALTY MODS:

Nitrous Oxide Systems polished bottle, APS stainless headers and turbo exhaust; RSR coil springs; Magnaflow performance mufflers; Sanyou model ECD T178DV sound system

WHEELS:

Veilside Andrew Evo with custom black-painted spokes, 19x9-inch front, 19x11-inch rear

TIRES:

Toyo T1R 245/40/ZR19 front, 285/35/ZR19 rear

PAINT:

House of Kolor Black with scarab graphics

DOUBLES CONSTRUCTED:

13 (2002, 2003, and 2004 models were used)

A Veilside body kit lends an even more muscular look to an already-fast car—Nissan's hi-po 350Z.

In addition to some horsepower upgrades, the DK 350Zs also got suspension modifications, like new sway bars and springs, to set them up for drifting. All cars also got new Nismo differentials to take higher horsepower and abuse.

2006 MAZDA RX-8

DRIVEN BY NEELA (PLAYED BY NATHALIE KELLEY)

>> Neela's blue and black RX-8 is not only beautiful to look at. The Mazda four-door rotary sports car is also built with near perfect 50:50 weight distribution, achieved in part by a lowered engine that has been set further back in the frame. Front-to-back balance is a handling advantage, but the RX-8 is actually a difficult car to drift. Good road-holding is essential in grip driving, but isn't what you want when your desired driving attitude is sideways.

Ramp up the power and rpms, though, and this hungry beast can go rim to rim with the best of them. RX-7s are an established part of the drift scene. So when real-world race driver Rod Millen decided to enter a realm his son, Rhys, had reached champion status in, he chose an RX-8. Neela pilots the same ride in *The Fast and the Furious Tokyo Drift*. She's not one to shrink from a challenge.

Neela's machine sports a paint job that goes from light to black, making the car look like it's emerging from darkness in each turn. Tinted windows add further mystery and make the impact that much greater when other drivers see that it's a woman who just drifted with the big boys. As the Drift King's girlfriend, she travels in tough company and being able to drive is essential to keeping pace and winning respect.

In the mountains, Neela proves that she and her RX-8 can confound physics and surf pavement like a pro. She shows that drifting is an art form, something complex and difficult whose champions make it look easy. In a parking lot, it's easy enough to hang the rear end out on a turn or two, but in mountain switchbacks it's the most dangerous way to the bottom of

the hill. In some ways, drifting is like martial arts—a study in supreme control, harnessing forces that can be dangerous—even deadly.

Neela's character represents the fact that while drifting is dominated by men, it's a sport in which women are starting to make their mark. Finesse and precision are hardly male talents alone, and with the right guidance—like that from the Drift King—a beautiful woman can become a formidable driver.

Neela's RX-8, like the other cars drifted in the film, was set up with appropriate wheels, tires, and suspension tweaks.

Because the setting for the film is Tokyo, the cars had to be right-hand drive. Buying them in Japan and bringing them over proved more cost effective than sourcing left-handers here and moving all the controls to the other side.

2006 MAZDA RX-8 SPECIFICATIONS

ENGINE:
Renesis 1.3-liter 13B rotary with GReddy turbo kit and e-management system; Tanabe exhaust system

BODY MODS:
Veilside body kit D1-GT, carbon fiber–painted cowl hood, and Veilside carbon fiber GT wing

INTERIOR:
Takata seat belts and Nardi steering wheel

SUSPENSION MODS:
Cusco LSD and rear swaybar; Tein coil springs

WHEELS:
Volk Racing GT-AV silver #0363, 19x18.5 front, 19x9.5 rear

TIRES:
Toyo Proxes, 245/35/ZR19 front, 255/30/ZR19 rear

PAINT COLOR:
House of Kolor Black, blue, light blue

DOUBLES CONSTRUCTED:
5 (2004, 2005, and 2006 models were used)

Neela knows how to drift like the big boys, so her car, like theirs, is an obvious and purposeful performance machine.

A Veilside body kit and carbon fiber wing complement the custom paint job to make Neela's car something special among other distinctive RX-8s.

The custom paint on the picture car is polished to a mirror gloss, as the front wheel reflected in the door demonstrates. A car that will go to promotions and shows will be built to perfection, while those used for stunts look different inside because safety takes top priority.

1994 VEILSIDE MAZDA RX-7

DRIVEN BY HAN (PLAYED BY SUNG KANG)

>> Mazda's awesome RX-7 twin-turbocharged rotary rocket is a mainstay in *The Fast and the Furious* films. The original king of the streets, Dominic Toretto, accepts all challenges in his red RX-7 in the first film, and in *2 Fast 2 Furious*, the RX-7 returns, this time piloted by Slap Jack. Though the paint, graphics, and body kits differ, the RX-7's sexy lines, excellent power, and top-notch handling remain unmistakable. From the moment it hit U.S. shores in third-generation guise, the RX-7 has been a wolf in wolf's clothing—a serious driving machine.

Five years after *The Fast and the Furious* chronicled L.A.'s street-racer scene, the RX-7 is still a force to be reckoned with, even in Japan, the wellspring of the affordable—and highly modifiable—sport compact car. Too sophisticated for American mechanics to keep up with, the third-generation car disappeared from U.S. shores after 1995. But in Japan, Mazda had no intention of abandoning its wondercar. It continued to tweak and refine the RX-7 to keep pace with other manufacturers intent on dominating the performance car culture.

The paint and body kit on Han's RX-7 make it the most distinctive example of the model in the three films, even though Dom Toretto's and Orange Julius's cars in the first two films also had custom graphics and body kits.

In *Initial D*, the manga and anime series that turned millions of young minds onto the drifting scene, the car that hero Tak Fujiwara confronts in his first big drift race is an RX-7. So it's only fitting that the car is featured in *The Fast and the Furious: Tokyo Drift*. Han, the Drift King's business partner (who's skimming some extra profits for himself), has a wicked RX-7 in addition to the Silvia Sean trashes in his first drifting misadventure against the Drift King. Toretto's car was an eye-grabber, Slap Jack's was all-sleek style, but Han's RX-7 is the most menacing of all, exuding the wind-cheating brawn of a full-on race car. When Sean and Han blow past a cop car, it doesn't even pull out. No point. The factory-tuned patrol car can't beat 180-kilometer-an-hour speed. That's Sunday-drive pace for Han's RX-7.

1994 VEILSIDE MAZDA RX-7 SPECIFICATIONS

ENGINE:
Veilside built with Apexera Power FC engine management system; HKS TO42 turbo kit and V-mounted intercooler; Veilside custom intercooler piping; NKG racing spark plugs

BODY MODS:
Veilside Fortune RX-7 body kit

INTERIOR:
Veilside console, audio board, tension bar, and D1R seats; Sparco seat belts and steering wheel

SUSPENSION MODS:
Apexera N1 dampner and Rotora brake system

WHEELS:
Veilside 19x9-inch front, 19x12-inch rear

TIRES:
Pirelli P Zero 255/30/ZR19 front, 305/25/ZR19 rear

PAINT:
House of Kolor black and orange

DOUBLES CONSTRUCTED:
9 (1992, 1993, and 1994 models were used)

The split-window bodywork on Han's RX-7 is very unique, evocative for old-school viewers of Chevrolet's 1963 Corvette coupe.

In the party scene that surrounds the car culture, good stereo sounds can be as important as a powerful engine.

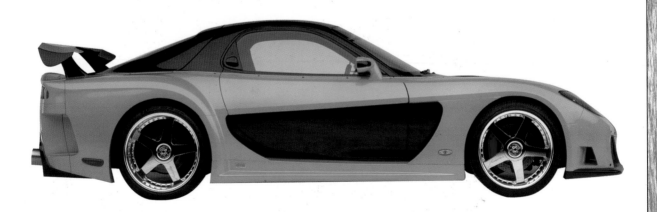

The original Veilside RX-7 used in *The Fast and the Furious: Tokyo Drift* was bought after it won the 2005 Tokyo Auto Salon best of show. After being shipped to the United States and repainted, it was used as stunt car because it was so powerful. Its rear end was replaced three times, but the car never crashed and the engine and transmission remained strong throughout the film.

2006 MITSUBISHI EVO IX

DRIVEN BY SEAN BOSWELL (PLAYED BY LUCAS BLACK)

>> At no point in developing the Lancer Evolution was Mitsubishi ever fooling around. The manufacturer's goal was to win the World Rally Championship with this car. Because of rally car racing rules, Mitsubishi had to offer the Evo in a street version for average Joe speed freaks. These vehicles were snapped up hungrily, proving a viable, eager market for a car that put performance above any other production criterion. Mitsubishi's rally ambitions paid a wonderful dividend to legions of street drivers: a reasonably priced car that could go to wheel-to-wheel with exotics costing as much as a driveway full of Evos.

The Evo debuted in *2 Fast 2 Furious* as Brian O'Conner's second car, coming on the scene after O'Conner's phenomenal Skyline GT-R gets taken out by police early on in the film. In *The Fast and the Furious: Tokyo Drift*, Sean Boswell gets an Evo after he destroys

Han's Silvia S-15. While it seems strange to reward a young man who has just destroyed one of your cars, Han is looking for an able employee and sees both skill and determination in the plucky American who takes on the Drift King in a competition he's never tried.

As soon as Han gives Sean the Evo's keys, Sean wants to learn how to drift it. First, they have to modify the car, including taking back some of its grip by changing it from all-wheel-drive to rear-wheel drive. Though he had a somewhat bitter taste of drifting at the wheel of the Silvia, Sean still needs time to synthesize a burnout and a fish-tail into the graceful slalom enthusiasts call drifting. It's slow going, and expensive in tires, but Sean's a natural wheelman. With the right coaching and machinery, he finds his slide.

Unfortunately, unlike the Evo VII in *2 Fast 2 Furious*, the IX doesn't make it out of the third film in one piece. Han has crossed DK by skimming profits from their partnership, and Sean has crossed DK by trying to win Neela. With DK's ties to the Yakuza crime machine, there's a price for wronging him. Fleeing a 350Z posse, Sean escapes in the Evo, but not without totaling it in the process.

Mitsubishi's Evo debuted in *2 Fast 2 Furious* as Brian O'Conner's second car. The Evo IX builds on its predecessor's all-out performance design.

Toyo decals feature on many of *The Fast and the Furious* cars—and justly so, as the company provided tires and plenty of technical assistance. There are few things harder on a tire than drifting, so the right tires—and plenty of them—were critical to the third film.

The roll cage is well padded to cushion the inevitable bumps between it and stunt drivers' arms, legs, and helmets.

Left: An aggressive front body kit gives Sean's Evo a pure competition look.

ENGINE:

2-liter, turbocharged, DOHC 4G63 engine in stock trim; RMR air intake system and downpipe

BODY MODS:

APR body kit and rear wing; APR Racing side mirrors

INTERIOR:

Recaro seats; Takata seat belts; Auto Meter gauges; APR carbon fiber instrument cluster; Matt Sweeny custom fabricated roll bar; Sparco steering wheel

WHEELS:

Ray's Wheels G-Games 99B,19x8.5-inch front and rear with 20-mm billet bolt on spacers

TIRES:

Toyo Proxes T1R 255/35/ZR19 front; 255/35/NR19 rear

PAINT:

House of Kolor Red with black graphics

DOUBLES CONSTRUCTED:

12

The illusion in car movies is that a single hero car propels its human star through all of the vehicle's stunts and races. In fact, the thrashing is shared among many cars—which are repaired by many mechanics. All seven of these Evos play one car on screen (and the Mustang at the end is also one of many).

To drift an otherwise four-wheel drive Evo requires disconnecting the front drive wheels.

Nineteen-inch wheels require low-profile tires, which may be good for cornering but provide little shock absorption for stunts and bumps.

2002 NISSAN 350Z

DRIVEN BY MORIMOTO (PLAYED BY LEONARDO NAM)

>> While Morimoto is the first Japanese drifter to speak to Sean in English, what he says is not welcoming. He wants Sean to stay away from Neela, the one person in his new home Sean is eager to get to know. Morimoto's an imposing guy and his crowd has little time for a transplanted American who doesn't know drifting from driftwood.

The Drift King leads the Tokyo drift crowd that Morimoto hangs with, and DK's ride choice, the 350Z, has been copied by others, including Morimoto. Nissan's broad, low heir to the 240Z legacy makes a menacing sight in numbers, cruising Tokyo's streets like a mechanized predator. Morimoto's Z gleams gold in profile but fades to black as the eye travels up the hood and top. In a rearview mirror, the car can be hard to see with its black hood until Morimoto puts it into a drift, when a flash of gold advertises its driver's sideways prowess.

Too bad the car is not enough when Morimoto takes on Sean in a challenge that had been building since their first encounter. Since then, Sean has been training with Han, expanding his inherent skills from straight-line grip driving to drifting's controlled chaos. At the wheel of Han's Evo, Sean out drifts Morimoto, taking some of the gleam from his car and his proud stare.

Morimoto's 350Z had one of the nicest paint jobs in the film.

Hood pins are a classic touch. They've anchored hoods to high-performance cars for decades, keeping the hoods firmly secured at high speeds.

Out back, prominent dual tail pipes are another hint that you're following a car that can get up and go. Note how far the wide body kit extends the quarter panels beyond the edge of the taillights.

ENGINE:

3.5-liter VQ35DE V-6

BODY MODS:

Top Secret wide body kit, hood, and rear wing; Speedway Engineering hood pins

INTERIOR:

Recaro black and gold seats; Takata MPH-340R seat belts; Sparco steering wheel

SPECIALTY MODS:

Nitrous Oxide Systems polished bottle

WHEELS:

Volk by Ray's GTC Gold Spoke, 18x9-inch front, 19x10.5-inch rear

TIRES:

Toyo T1R 255/40/ZR18 front, 275/35/ZR19 rear

PAINT:

House of Kolor gold and black

DOUBLES CONSTRUCTED:

6

For extra juice, Morimoto's Z was built up with an HKS supercharger to make about 360-370 horsepower at the rear wheels. A NOS nitrous bottle furthered the performance touch.

Custom wheels are as important in distinguishing the cars as body kits and paint. These also provide for easy assessment of the pads and rotors—components pushed hard in the *The Fast and the Furious* films.

The nose piece on the Top Secret wide body kit fitted to Morimoto's 350Z extends the front of the car and sharpens its profile.

1993 NISSAN SILVIA S-13

DRIVEN BY VIRGIL *(PLAYED BY JASON TOBIN)*

>> The Silvia first appeared in 1964 at the Tokyo Motor Show as a sporting coupe. The first year's model bore front disc brakes and handmade body panels. Though stylish, the original model was never put into large-scale production. In 1974, the company reintroduced the Silvia with a larger production and sales vision under the S10 designation (this numbering system would continue throughout future models). And more than a decade later, as drifting began to take hold in Japan, its practitioners—trying the new art form in whatever vehicles they had available— found a winner in the Silvia.

With high horsepower and rear-wheel drive, the Silvia S-13 makes an excellent drift car, especially the turbocharged K version. The car was an important player when U.S. drivers began to enter the competitive drifting scene. Many U.S. D1 Grand Prix drivers campaigned the S-13. Because of its prowess, the car is well served by the aftermarket and amenable to a broad range of tweaking, both in looks and performance.

Virgil, one of Han's friends and mechanics in *The Fast and the Furious: Tokyo Drift*, is an ace with a wrench, so we know his S-13 is well tuned for its job. When Han's Evo, the one Sean had been relying on and learned to drift in, gets destroyed, Virgil lends Sean a hand. Sean needs all the help he can get in his drift race against DK.

ENGINE:
2-liter, DOHC, turbocharged 16-valve SR20DET 4-cylinder

BODY MODS:
C-West GT carbon 1 wing

INTERIOR:
Sparco Corsa black seats and Sparco seat belts

WHEELS:
Ray's Gram Lights 57 Pro, 17x8-inch front, 17x9-inch rear

TIRES:
Toyo Proxes 225/45/ZR17 front, 235/40/ZR17 rear

PAINT:
House of Kolor Blue with white stripes; DRFT logo on hood and doors

DOUBLES CONSTRUCTED:
2

The C-West wing is thick and rigid enough that it can be supported toward the center on stout struts.

2003 NISSAN 350Z

DRIVEN BY TEA HAIR

>> The 350Z is a lineal descendent of the remarkable 240Z, which stormed U.S. shores at the beginning of the 1970s. With distinctive looks and a guttural straight-six engine, the 240Z found an instant following among sports car enthusiasts looking for something more nimble than the straight-line muscle cars Detroit was turning out. The Z evolved into the 1990s, growing more advanced, more luxurious, and more expensive until the motorsports-minded young people who were the Z's greatest proponents could no longer afford the car their demographic had made so popular. By 1996, the original Z had run its course.

Luckily, Nissan did not forget the car and the symbol that were so important to its U.S.—and world—presence. The company introduced the new 350Z in 2002 to widespread accolades. Handsome, reasonably priced, and a performance powerhouse, the 350Z carries on the sporting prowess the first Z introduced.

It's no coincidence that young performance enthusiasts are drawn to the 350Z. With great power and a certain menace, the 350Z is a perfect car for the Drift King, his strong-arm Morimoto, and associate Tea Hair. Their three cars together highlight the Z's stealthy appeal, while demonstrating the many striking and varied looks young enthusiasts can achieve with their cars.

For DK and his friends, the production needed a good supply of right-hand drive 350Zs. Fortunately, a single supplier in Japan had enough cars on hand to meet the film's Z needs.

Using a pack of 350Zs gave DK and his crew an extra sense of power and danger, yet it was important to make each car distinct. Tea Hair's Z uses a body kit from Top Secret, a Japanese supplier that provided a lot of support to the third film.

ENGINE:

3.5-liter VQ35DE V-6

BODY MODS:

Top Secret body kit and GT rear wing; Top Secret carbon fiber–painted hood; Speedway Engineering hood pins

INTERIOR:

Takata seat belts; Sparco blue steering wheel

SPECIALTY MODS:

Nitrous Oxide Systems blue bottle

WHEELS:

Volk Racing GT-C silver No. 0351 18x9-inch front, 18x10-inch rear

TIRES:

Toyo Proxes 245/40/ZR18 front, 275/35/ZR18 rear

PAINT:

House of Kolor Silver and blue

DOUBLES CONSTRUCTED:

2

Tea Hair's Z has a different Top Secret body kit from the one used on Morimoto's car. Tea Hair's fender flares pretty much fit within the rear wing, while Morimoto's stand proud of the wing.

Yet another take on the tough, five-spoke wheel seen on many of the third film's cars.

A lot of time and talent goes into designing the paint and graphics for these cars. Fans have duplicated cars from the first two films and no doubt will do so with the third.

1967 FORD MUSTANG

OWNED BY SERGEANT MAJOR BOSWELL (PLAYED BY BRIAN GOODMAN) AND DRIVEN BY SEAN BOSWELL

>> When Sean gets to Tokyo and sees his father's cramped quarters, which he will share, his enthusiasm for his new home isn't great. It also doesn't help that his father, a U.S. Army sergeant major, doesn't mind a drink and has never had much time for his son. And on top of that, Sean's need to come here for screwing up again back in the United States hasn't put his arrival in an auspicious light either.

Yet Sean's father does have something he can appreciate: an American car that has seen better days. Sean turned his Monte Carlo into a quarter-mile contender before destroying it and his future back home, so he is more than interested in his father's past-prime Mustang fastback. Like Sean, it's seen some hard miles, but also has character and potential. Both could perform at a much higher level, given the right chance.

Sean's father found the car dusty and unwanted at the army base. In a world of small, nimble, more fuel-efficient machines, no one was much interested in the 1967 Ford. But Sean got his appreciation for old iron from somebody.

Sergeant Boswell saved the Mustang from the crusher and now has it in a garage near his home. It's the first thing Sean sees that gives him a sense of hope.

The Mustang isn't ready when he first sees it; its engine hasn't turned in a long time. In a reversal of the traditional engine swap—out with the old four or six-banger, in with the V-8—the Mustang finds new life with a modern powerplant: the modified RB26 from Han's demolished Silvia S-15. Sean and friends also modify the suspension, fitting Global West control arms and front coilovers and KYB rear shocks. They upgrade the brakes from antiquated Ford items to Wilwood disks.

Swapping Silvia parts into a classic Mustang might baffle traditional enthusiasts of both Japanese and American iron, but the move suits Sean and the story. The original Mustang lump is inoperable and if the Drift King thinks Sean's hopelessly outgunned in their final showdown, all the better for the underdog. The mix of old and new parts, and different cultures, also parallels Sean's battles to get along with his father and fit into his new country's highly competitive drift scene. The hybrid Mustang combines Sean's father's interests with his own and echoes the theme of displaced youths finding meaning by pushing limits at the wheel of an automobile.

Hot rodders have been throwing newer engines in classic cars for decades, but few if any had swapped in a top-flight Japanese powerplant before *The Fast and the Furious: Tokyo Drift* team built this Mustang.

Shelby-style stripes advertise the Mustang's racing connections.

ENGINE:
Transplanted Nissan Skyline GT-R RB26 turbocharged six-cylinder with Earl's Performance steel braided line and anodized fittings; Be Cool aluminum radiator

BODY MODS:
Shelby-style B-pillar scoops

INTERIOR:
Auto meter gauges; custom-fabricated roll bar; Hurst shifter; Flaming River steering wheel; Diest Seat Belts

WHEELS:
Volk Racing grey GT-7 No. 0355, 19x9-inch front, 19x10-inch rear

TIRES:
Toyo Proxes 245/35/ZR19 front, 275/35/ZR19 rear

SUSPENSION MODS:
Global West control arms and front coilovers; KYB rear shocks; Wilwood disc brakes

PAINT COLOR:
House of Kolor Green with white stripes

DOUBLES CONSTRUCTED:
7

A tuner-style wide-mouth exhaust is one of the few clues that this is no ordinary Mustang.

A powerful Skyline straight-six fitted with single turbocharger had ample room under the Mustang's hood. Since the engine came from a four-wheel drive Skyline, it is mated to an older, rear-wheel drive Skyline transmission. This was the hardest car in the film to set up for drifting at the level the stunt drivers required.

The Mustang wears the seven-spoke wheels of Han's Silvia, which donated its previously transplanted Nissan Skyline engine.

This graceful profile is what leads many fans to dub the '67 their favorite Mustang of all.

GET THE DRIFT

>> If it has wheels, people will race it—and sometimes even wheels aren't a requirement. Yet racing is not the only thrilling, challenging way to hurl an automobile over an expanse of tarmac. Drifting shares some of racing's exciting features, like incredible driver skill and—at its highest levels—beautiful, powerful, finely-tuned machines. But drifting is not about speed. Like exciting freestyle competitions in sports such as skateboarding, skiing, skating, and BMX, drifting is about style. Speed plays a part, as in those sports, but the quickest time is not the main objective.

Though it has much in common with "grip" contests, like road racing, drifting inverts one of racing's fundamental premises: that maximum traction is the key to success. The essence of drifting is to avoid traction and if there's no tire slip at all, you're not drifting. Racers push the limits of adhesion, trying to go as fast as possible without breaking the tires free. Drifters want the back tires to churn furiously and produce a fog of smoke—the more the better. And that's just the start.

The second critical component in drifting—the one the name evokes—is to move the car around the course with "angle." Drifters rarely look straight out the windshield and over the hood. That's because in a drift, the nose of the car does not point in the direction the car is moving. The driver watches the course looking out the passenger

"Angle," which crowds and the judges want to see, is how far sideways you can get the drift car while maintaining complete control. *Marc Urbano*

side of the windshield, the driver side window, or the passenger side window, with the rear of the car hanging out—way out—as if challenging the front end for the lead. While judges look for many things from a driver, they and the crowds love to see the back end hang the car almost sideways as it drifts around the course. Other attributes, like entry speed, maintaining the drift throughout the turn, and smoothly linking one turn to the next, are also important.

Just who invented drifting is hard to say, but it emerged as a sport in Japan in the 1980s. The man most closely associated with its origins is Keiichi Tsuchiya, known throughout the scene as the Drift King. The oft told story is that Keiichi

Tsuiso, or "twin battle," is a crowd favorite that demands incredible control and no small amount of nerve from the driver. It looks like a cooperative effort, but each driver is trying to look good while keeping his competitor from doing so. *Marc Urbano*

honed his driving skills on Japan's winding mountain roads. There, he practiced the technique of swinging out the back end of the car on tight turns. When he later entered a road racing career, he applied the same technique. He enjoyed some success at the wheel, but what really caught the public's eye were his high-speed drift turns. They were fresh and exciting; people wanted to see more of that style of driving.

Later a manga (comic book) series called *Initial-D* focused on drifting, bringing the sport to a wider, international audience. Widely popular, *Initial-D* also became an anime (cartoon) series and then a live-action film of the same name. Keiichi is mentioned in the anime series and his "Drift Bible" is now a touchstone reference for the sport. Millions of gamers around the world have also entered the drift enthusiasts' fold through hard-fought competition in cyberspace.

Drifting's graceful arcs belie the skill its artists possess. Cars are built to go where they're pointed—that's pretty much criterion number one for any other driver. To overcome that basic design parameter takes technique, horsepower, and a certain conspiratorial alliance with laws of physics the car's engineers set out to tame. Exactly what is happening when the car is pointing one way and going another—its wheels whirring at a speed that isn't reflected in the speedometer and the rear tires fighting to track a line different from the one the car is moving along—is hard to say. Video game developers, with all their technical and scientific prowess, were confounded in their early efforts to translate these competing forces into a model that made for realistic and consistent play. What's clear is that this sport ain't easy—which is a big reason fans love the way the best drivers make it look like it is.

Cars don't go into a drift with a gentle turn of the wheel. They have to be unsettled from the pavement with something stronger. Drivers have to overcome the tires' grip with momentum, horsepower, braking, clutching, a gear change, or a combination of these forces. First-time drifters are often befuddled by what it takes to get a car into a drift—and keep it there. Just like competitive grip driving, drifting requires pushing limits. Push too weak and you have no drift. Push too hard and you spin out, your car too often becoming intimate with a guardrail.

Drifting is all about the turns and coming in fast. The lead car is set up and starting to drift while the white RX-7 comes in at speed. *Marc Urbano*

Over the years, the many techniques enthusiasts have developed to initiate a drift have developed their own names, which no doubt vary some by locale. Drift Session, a promoter of the sport in Hawaii, lists a dozen techniques, including power over, E-brake drift, clutch kick, shift lock drift, dirt drop drift, feint drift, jump drift, braking drift, kansei drift, long slide drift, and swaying drift. The feint drift, a rally technique, uses momentum. The E-brake drift is similar to the snowy parking lot move in a front-wheel-drive car, where you put the back wheels into a slide by slowing them with the emergency brake.

Some techniques are a little more daring and may be banned at some venues. The dirt-drop drift involves putting the rear tires off the road and into loose gravel to break them free. The jump drift uses a curb for the same purpose.

One of the appealing aspects of the sport is that it doesn't cost too much to get involved. A rear-wheel-drive Japanese sport compact car is a typical starting point, but enthusiasts say almost any vehicle can be put into a drift. Some are better than others, though. Rear-wheel-drive vehicles are overwhelmingly preferred because disrupting traction in the rear tires is essential in drifting; there are many more ways to do this when these are the drive wheels. Front-wheel-drive drifting relies mainly on the handbrake with the drive wheels working to pull the car out of the drift.

Japanese cars are preferable because they are well served by the aftermarket. However, with drifting's rising popularity, the number of suitable, cheap cars is dwindling. An inexpensive car is the best starting point because beginners—and even pros—break things from time to time. And even with no breakage, drifting eats tires.

Popular drifting competitions today include solo driving and tsuiso, or "twin battle." The solo contests are judged on each driver's technique on the course, with such elements as entry speed, the "line" through turns, angle, tire smoke, smoothness, and more subjective criteria, like flair, going to a driver's score. The tsuiso features two cars at once, one leading, one pursuing. The object is to emphasize your own drifting skills while at the same time strategically preventing your competitor from doing the same through your speed and location.

Drifting has an accessible, grassroots feel, which is open to new drivers and fans alike, including women. That's part of its appeal, and the way many weekend warriors hope it remains.

A good drifting car has plenty of torque on tap to overcome friction and get the back wheels spinning and smoking, even when the turn is not very sharp. *Marc Urbano*

THE EXTRAS

"That's my car right. . . there"

>> Just as movies have human extras—with script names like WAITRESS TWO or MAN WITH SURFBOARD—car movies involve vehicles that fill in the background or make brief appearances in chases, at the curb or in a garage. *The Fast and the Furious* movies included hundreds of car extras, as well as cars driven by featured characters with only a brief time on screen.

In the first film, Jesse's Jetta has a small but meaningful role. Jesse, played by Chad Lindberg, is Dom Toretto's technical wiz, who helps spec and build O'Conner's Supra. His Jetta is fast, but not fast enough to beat Johnny Tran's black Honda S2000. When he loses the race, and his pink slip, Jesse flees, bringing Tran (Rick Yune) and a flurry of machine-gun fire back to Toretto's.

According to technical advisor Craig Lieberman, the Jetta had a two-liter, four-cylinder lump mated to an automatic transmission. The car was also fitted with nitrous for a little more zip. For a more aggressive exhaust note, producers swapped in the sound of a turbo Integra race car.

Though longer and heavier than many of its peers, the Toyota Chaser is a favorite among drifters.

Another cool but briefly shown car in the first film is a Nissan Maxima driven by Vince, played by Matt Schulze. The car sports metallic-blue paint, a Stillen body kit with side-exit exhaust, a Veilside rear spoiler, and HP Racing Flight wheels. Underhood and undercarriage mods include a Vortech supercharger, plus a bevy of performance parts from Stillen, including intake, exhaust, brake system, strut tower bars, sway bar, struts, and

As a high-powered, rear-engine car in stock trim, the Chaser received few modifications for filming. Custom paint, GT wing, tinted windows, and Volk GT-V racing wheels gave the car the right look.

springs. Though not featured in the film, the Maxima's entertainment system boasts triple JBL subwoofers, five JBL amplifiers, Infiniti speakers, inboard Sony PlayStation, two color monitors, CD player, and many other goodies.

Dozens of other cars—many driven by their owners—helped to create the street-race atmosphere and provided a strong sense of realism. Enthusiasts were so excited about a film focused on their passion that they showed up on location by the hundreds for a chance to get into a scene with their cars.

The third film was no different, relying on background vehicles to complete the look of large car gatherings. Because of the Tokyo setting, any car seen had to be right-handed drive. Of course, every vehicle used for stunts or other fast driving has to be prepared to ensure that it can hold up to shooting demands and protect its drivers and passengers. Cars like the Toyota Chaser and RX-7 used in the underground garage drift race were modified to drift well and safely. Twinkie's Volkswagen Touran Van, which features an Incredible Hulk–themed design, has a larger role, representing the party atmosphere present at drifting events.

Although not all of the cars that appear in each film will go on to be reproduced by fans and as toys, each vehicle has a part to play in making the story world come alive.

ACKNOWLEDGMENTS

>> Many busy, talented, and successful people generously shared their time and expertise with me over the course of this project. The best stuff comes from them; any errors are mine.

Thanks to Justin Lin, Dennis McCarthy, Eddie Paul, Craig Lieberman, and David Marder for their insights into the making of these exciting car movies and the vehicles and stunts involved. Eddie provided a nice foundation for the book in his prior writings and work on the films, and Craig supplied many cool details for captions and various entries from his immersion in the films and the import tuner scene. Dennis reviewed the manuscript and updated car specs. Antonio Alvendia kindly shared his in-depth knowledge of drifting.

A lot of people at Universal Studios and MBI Publishing Company also gathered essential resources and put valuable time and effort into this book. They include Cindy Chang, Veronika Beltran, Colleen Foster, and Carol McConnaughey, and ace editors Lee Klancher and Leah Noel.

Behind most writers with a roof over their heads and the occasional hot meal, there is also a successful and tolerant spouse. Thanks Jenneane. I love you, and our creditors are big fans, too.

In a broader sense, these films and this book about them derive from the efforts of hundreds of people who provided technical, artistic, mechanical, and administrative expertise to make it all come together on film. You know who you are and that your work was invaluable. Everyone who enjoys these films and the cars they feature is thankful for your labors.

— Kris Palmer, 2006

INDEX